A History of
BRITAIN
in
JUST A MINUTE

Gyles Brandreth

Just A Minute created by Ian Messiter

Illustrations by Steven Appleby

Last Word by Sue Perkins

BBC
BOOKS

BBC Books, an imprint of Ebury Publishing
20 Vauxhall Bridge Road,
London SW1V 2SA

BBC Books is part of the Penguin Random House group of companies
whose addresses can be found at global.penguinrandomhouse.com

Penguin
Random House
UK

This book is published to accompany the radio series entitled *Just A Minute*,
created by Ian Messiter and broadcast on BBC Radio 4.

First published by BBC Books in 2022

www.penguin.co.uk

A CIP catalogue record for this book is available from the British Library

ISBN 9781785947599

Printed and bound in Great Britain by Clays Ltd, Elcograf S.p.A.

MIX
Paper from
responsible sources
FSC® C018179

CONTENTS

BEFORE...

silence

DURING...

speaking
for one
minute

AFTER...

What I just
said is now
in the
past.

It's history.

JUST A MINUTE – IN JUST A MINUTE

Depending on the speed at which you speak, you can deliver between 150 and 250 words in just a minute. This, then, is a quick-fire history of Just A Minute, *presented in 229 words, without hesitation, repetition or deviation.*

Just A Minute is a radio panel game devised by one of the great wireless producers of the twentieth century: the late Ian Messiter (1920–99). The idea, he claimed, came to him on the top of a Number 13 bus, when suddenly he recalled one Percival Parry Jones, a history master from his schooldays, who, catching the boy daydreaming in class, instructed him to repeat everything the teacher had said in the previous minute without hesitation or repetition. Adding 'deviation' as an extra offence, Messie – as he liked to be called* – used the format first in the fifties in a show called *One Minute, Please*, chaired by another of the broadcasting greats: Roy Plomley, the inventor of *Desert Island Discs*. The pilot for *Just A Minute* was recorded in 1967, featuring Clement Freud, Derek Nimmo, Beryl Reid and Wilma Ewart as the panellists, with Nicholas Parsons (1923 to two thousand and 20†) in the chair. Nick went on to helm *Just A Minute* for 52 years.

Sue Perkins is now in command of the good ship *Just A Minute*, but as the programme approaches its one-thousandth episode, not much else has changed – including the theme tune: Frederic Chopin's piano Waltz in D flat major, Op. 64, No. 1, nicknamed the 'Minute Waltz', not because it lasts that long (it doesn't: it's longer) but because it's very small!‡

---

* He didn't – but at least it avoids repeating 'Messiter'.

† Ingenious avoidance of twenty in '2020'.

‡ 'Cut out all these exclamation points. An exclamation point is like laughing at your own joke.' – F. Scott Fitzgerald.

HOW TO USE THIS BOOK

That's entirely up to you, of course, and that wobbly table has needed stabilising for years, so if this volume is the wedge you need, so be it. Alternatively, this could be the book that gets you through GCSE History with grades others can only dream of. My hope, of course, is that as well as devouring the book from cover to cover, before storing it in that special collection in your smallest room or upcycling it down at the charity shop, you will use it as a springboard to play *The History of Britain in Just A Minute* as a parlour game at home.

How does that work then?

In the radio version of *Just A Minute*, there is one chair, one whistle-blower and four players. At home, you need just one chair and you can have any number of players. On the radio, we manage to play around eight rounds in half an hour. At home, you can do as you please.

First, choose a chair and equip them with a stopwatch and a whistle.

The chair then opens the book at random and announces the title of the first subject that catches their eye.

The tallest player talks first and keeps talking for up to 60 seconds – either until the chair blows the whistle because one minute is up, or until one of the other players interrupts with a challenge.

The challenge will be allowed or disallowed by the chair. If it's allowed, the challenger gets a point and takes over the subject. If the challenge is disallowed, the player who was interrupted gets the point and continues with the subject. There is an extra point for speaking as the whistle blows and another point on top of that if you manage to speak for 60 seconds without interruption.

At the discretion of the chair, extra points can be given for wit, wisdom and historical erudition.

At the end of each round, the player with the lowest score at that point reads out the minute's worth on the chosen subject from the book – and the players can all agree that they're much better at playing the game than we are.

Then the book is closed and opened again at random and another subject is chosen. And so on, until you've had enough. (Though can you ever have enough of a good thing? I am hoping we can persuade the publishers to bring out *The History of the World in Just A Minute* in due course.)

You know the rules –

+ You must try to speak on the subject in the heading for just a minute.
+ You can repeat the words in the heading as often you like.
+ You can repeat little words – like 'and' and 'but' and 'the' and even 'you' and 'I' and 'like' itself – but watch how you go. (The way 'like', like, crops up in the discourse on *Love Island*, like, is probably excessive, like.) If challenged, the chair's decision is final.
+ Hesitation is … er … just that.
+ Deviation is talking about anything that isn't directly related to the subject in the heading. Deviation can also include deviating from the norms of good English. Obviously, if the subject heading is 'Old English Proverbs', saying that a slight inclination of the cranium is an adequate substitution for a momentary closure of one optic to an equine quadruped utterly devoid of any visionary capacity is a legitimate way of expressing the notion that a nod's as good as a wink to a blind horse: it's not deviation. Veering into *non sequiturs* and gobbledygook is.

In playing the 240 or so rounds in this book I have done my best to stick to the rules. Keeping an eye on me has been my publisher's whistle-blower and he has added notes at the foot of most pages giving both his assessment of my performance and general guidance on *JAM* technique. Of course, the joy of *Just A Minute* is that every player plays it differently. I do it my way. You will do it yours. After all, you are unique – just like everyone else.

WELCOME TO THE HISTORY OF BRITAIN IN JUST A MINUTE ...

... and as the 'Minute Waltz' fades away (at least in your head I hope it does because a Chopin earworm can be less than soothing), it's my huge pleasure to welcome you to *The History of Britain in Just A Minute,* in which I, Gyles Brandreth (who has been playing the game since 1982), will be joining a select gallimaufry of fabulous fellow players in 240 rounds of our favourite word game in the hope of telling you, vividly, if not always entirely accurately, our extraordinary island story – and encapsulating the very essence of Britishness – from prehistoric times to the present day, and doing so, of course, without hesitation, deviation or repetition. Yes, I know I have used the word 'game' twice already – and now the word 'word' four times in all – but we haven't started yet. (And 'I' has cropped up quite a bit already, too, but as a rule little words like 'I' and 'and' don't count. 'Already' does count, however, and I have used that a couple of times already. It's not as easy as it looks, is it?)

Our aim has been to produce a volume that will tell you all you'll ever need to know about Britain and the British way of life. This is the book we hope incoming ambassadors will be given to introduce them to our country's heritage and customs. There is a definite possibility of that because it just so happens that our next sovereign is a *Just A Minute* aficionado. We all knew that as a boy Prince Charles was a fan of the madcap humour of *The Goons* – to the extent that Spike Milligan once repaid a royal compliment by calling the heir to the throne 'a grovelling bastard' – but it wasn't until *Just A Minute*'s fiftieth birthday that we discovered that the Prince of Wales is also a *JAM* devotee. To mark our Golden Jubilee, Prince Charles appeared on the show and revealed that he doesn't just love the programme, he plays the game, too, leaving messages on his sons' phones in *Just A Minute* style, without hesitation, deviation or repetition.

The Duchess of Cornwall is also an avid listener. I found that out the hard way. Once on the programme, challenged to talk about 'My Secret Crush', I conjured up an elaborate 60-second fantasy involving an imagined encounter with the young Camilla in her jodhpurs smoking her Woodbines behind the stables … only to meet Her Royal Highness shortly after the broadcast and discover that she had been listening. She conceded she might have been smoking, but insisted they wouldn't have been Woodbines.

Like the Royal Family, *Just A Minute* is a very British institution. To echo another British broadcasting institution (*Listen With Mother* – see page 204), 'Are you sitting comfortably? Then we'll begin.'

Sit on me!

The TIMELINE of HISTORY

THE FIRST HUMANS.

TO THE PAST...

Stories painted on cave walls.

Stories turned into songs.

Stories turned into religions.

Stories told around camp fires.

Stories turned into fairy tales.

Events half remembered.

Events misremembered.

Events made up.

Forgotten.

Rumour.

Hearsay.

Events told by the victors.

Imagined.

Events printed in books.

Events told by the losers.

Events written down by someone who wasn't there.

Events photographed.

Filmed.

Fabricated.

Faked.

Re-edited.

Recreated as entertainment.

Made for television.

1

In the Beginning ...

TO THE
FUTURE...

WHEN BRITAIN BECAME AN ISLAND

When you think of the big imponderable questions of our time –
If music be the food of love, why can't rabbits play the ukulele?
What did the fellow who invented the drawing board go back
to? – none is bigger nor more challenging than the question:
when exactly did Britain become an island?* No one knows for
sure, but according to most reliable source available – the British
Broadcasting Corporation† News website – the coastline of what
would become modern Britain began to emerge at the end of the
last Ice Age around 10,000 years ago. What we call the Irish Sea,
the North one and the English Channel were all rock solid until
the frozen stuff melted and water levels rose. Then in 6100 BC a
terrific tsunami from around what's now Norway cascaded south
and finished the job. Britain broke free of mainland Europe for
good and Nigel Farage's Neanderthal forebears threw their clubs
in the air with delight.

---

* **D** Posing rhetorical questions requires careful handling, where they risk
being challenged for deviation. However, they can work as effective tactics to
divert the reader from what is being said, while you assemble an answer and
the words with which to express it.

† **R** The mark of a seasoned player here. 'BBC' is one of the commonest
banana skins for contestants, but for the keen-eared it represents an obvious
repetition of the letter B.

WHAT I KNOW ABOUT THE BEAKERS

Are we thinking here about Dr Beaker, the fellow who discovered sodium? Na! Or Dr Bunsen Honeydew's assistant in *The Muppets*? Or Jacqueline Wilson's great creation, Tracy Beaker? Or even that fine blues guitarist, Norman Beaker, whose real name wasn't actually Beaker but Hume?* None of the aforementioned, I imagine, because this is *The History of Britain in Just A Minute* so the Beakers we're on about are the folk who migrated to our part of the world from central Europe and settled here around 4400 years ago. They replaced the descendants of Cheddar Man who had been a big cheese in his day, but whose time was long gone.† A beaker, as you know, is a kind of drinking vessel and the Beakers are so called because the archaeologists tell us they arrived bringing stoneware beakers with them. The Tupperware people are a different thing altogether.‡

BEAKER PEOPLE COMPLETE
DINNER SERVICE c. 3000 BC

← NAPKIN RING

---

* **D** The wild names of blues musicians offer an example of an opportunity for undetected deviation: Norman Beaker happens to be real, but which of these is real: Howlin' Dog Peters, Curly Legs McGinty, Fat Lemon Hopkins? The answer: none of them. See also: eighteenth-century prime ministers, who have names like the Earl of Cribbage.

† **D** Some might challenge here on the grounds that if his time was long gone this constitutes deviation. However, with a pedigree of our own stretching back over half-a-century, we take the long view on *Just A Minute*. For us, the past is always present and Cheddar Man survives, so called because he was excavated in 1903 in the Cheddar Gorge in Somerset, and as such is Britain's oldest complete human skeleton and reckoned to date back more than 9000 years.

‡ **D** A challenge for deviation might legitimately be made and, coming right at the end of the minute's allowance, it would be a winner. In the interests of exegesis, however, the Tupperware people did exist. They were the colleagues of Earl Tupper who invented the original Tupperware container in PE, USA, in 1942.

THE TRUTH ABOUT STONEHENGE

The truth about Stonehenge is the parking is a nightmare. It's been there, this Stonehenge thing, a scheduled ancient monument, a World Heritage site, on the A303 just outside Amesbury in Wiltshire, for four thousand years, possibly five – you'd have thought they could have got that sorted by now, but no. And don't get me started on the toilets. There aren't any. Turn up in your druid's rigout at the crack of dawn ready to see in the summer solstice on a chilly June morning and, what with the rising dew and the descending drizzle, and the half-hour tramp from wherever you've managed to park your car and, believe me, you'll find you're frantic for a wee way before the sun rises behind the Heel Stone in the northeast part of the horizon and its first rays shine into the heart of Stonehenge, that mystic collection of mysterious stones that might be the *locus* of a primordial burial ground or some huge, elaborate prehistoric sundial. Who cares? There are absolutely no facilities. It's a bloody disgrace.

ANCIENT STONE-AGE FAMILY
SALOON WITH NOWHERE TO PARK
ABANDONED IN A FIELD.

THE BRONZE AGE

The Bronze Age followed the Ambre Solaire Age, then the Tanning Salon Age, in a seamless (yes, we're talking all-over body exposure here) shift to the new era. This spread throughout Europe after people got serious about it on the island of Crete, where visitors from southern Russia arrived around 2000 BC. They brought familiar things from home: borscht, blinis, vodka, *Pravda* and a new kind of substance that was sooooooo much better than anything anyone had been using until then to get stoned. Dealers found that combining tin with copper gave you a cutting-edge fix that kept you sharp and was seriously cool. Both materials were readily available in Britain and when bronzed travellers pitched up on these shores, their new look took off big-time. Bronze was everywhere. Weapons were forged from it, so were tools like axes, which made it easier to clear ground for agriculture – the innovative way of providing food that didn't involve scary stand-offs with massive mastodons, and scratching around for nuts and berries – or even the occasional magic mushroom.

I'M A CELT

'I'm a cult!' was a favourite cry of the late, great comic actor, writer and entertainer, Kenneth Williams, for many years one of the stalwarts and star attractions of *Just A Minute* on Radio 4.* 'I'm a Celt!' on the other hand is an exclamation you might hear falling from the snarling lips of an angry Scottish football player if you suggested he played for the Hamilton Academicals or the Arbroath Smokies when in fact he's the captain of Glasgow Celtic. 'I'm a Celt!' is not something you'd hear a true Celt saying, because the ancient Celts didn't speak English. They spoke an assortment of languages, some of which have survived, like Gaelic – not to be confused with garlic, the preferred herb of those of Celt heritage who came from Brittany. The ones who settled in the British Isles dropped their roots in Ireland, Scotland, Wales, Cornwall and the Isle of Man. The Celts were a very advanced society and famous for doing all their own laundry, which is why we call the time they lived in 'the Iron Age'.

---

* Running close to a challenge for deviation here. But the clever move has been to focus on the past stalwart of the show (Kenneth Williams) and to use the name, *Just A Minute*, as a distraction. Keen followers of the game's tactics and subterfuges will spot that almost 20 per cent of the designated time has been used already.

JULIUS CAESAR THE ROMAN GEEZER

The name 'Celts' is used to describe people who lived in Britain and northwest Europe during the Iron Age – from around 600 BC for about half a millennium until the Romans arrived led by Julius Caesar the Roman geezer who famously squashed his nose in a lemon squeezer. That happened while Caesar was making the salad dressing for which he is now so famous and got involved in a dispute with his brother Waldorf over who owned the rights in the recipe – Julius, Waldo or Paul Newman. Julius Caesar first landed on our shores on 26 August 55 BCE – that's Before the Common Era because I don't fancy repeating the second and third letters of the alphabet just now – but it was almost another century before Rome actually conquered Britain in AD 43 – that's Anno Domini, 'in the year of Our Lord' (you see I'm mixing it up a bit). Julius would have stayed longer but turned back when a local soothsayer warned him off visiting a dangerous family in Cambridgeshire: 'Beware the Ides of March.' According to Asterix the Gaul, not a reliable historian, Caesar overwhelmed us because the ancient Britons stopped fighting every afternoon for a cup of hot water with milk, tea not yet having been brought to the country. In fact, Caesar came, saw and then conked out. On the day of his funeral his mate Mark Antony came to Bury. He then travelled on to Accrington, Clitheroe and Lytham St Annes.

Ouch...

Can't believe I just did that...

clearly a faulty lemon squeezer, sire.

THE BEAUTY OF BOUDICCA

Boudicca, an Iron Age queen from East Anglia, enjoyed a second round of fame centuries later when Edwardian suffragettes adopted her as an icon of women's lib – and the beauty of Boudicca* is that we know a lot about her, even if much of it is nonsense. She didn't arm the wheels of her war chariots with scythes: the sculptor of her Embankment statue cribbed the idea from ancient Persia. Nor did Boudicca make her rousing speeches to rally the troops, or if she exhorted them, who knows what she said? However, Tacitus had the eyewitness account of his father-in-law, who served in Britain when Boudicca led an East Anglian uprising that trashed Colchester, London and St Albans. This old British sovereign had no time for the Treaty of Rome. She had even less for the Eurocentric bureaucracy that governed the lives of her Iceni people. An assault by Latin louts was the final straw and around AD 60 the rebellion erupted, blowing away everything in its wake, including the 9th Legion, before the Italian defence got its act together in the second half and emerged the winner at full time.

---

* There's an interesting split at play in this entry. The last word of the topic becomes the first word in the delivery, a ploy which leads would-be challengers to deduce subconsciously that the subject is being fully addressed. In actual fact, approaching a fifth of the topic is discussed before the full wording is given. This suggests that the player has cleverly avoided being challenged for hesitation while scrambling for a suitable answer.

JOSIE LAWRENCE ON ...
THE BEAUTY OF BOUDICCA*

Let me tell you now of the beauty of Boudicca, Queen of the Iceni. Boudicca was a striking female to behold, tall and powerful. Her sheer charisma and size drew sighs from her followers.† Boudicca had long, flaming-red hair and the most beautiful, penetrating eyes. Her face was often daubed in blue woad given to her by the L'Oréal tribe because she was worth it. Boudicca's body would always be adorned in gold and silver rings, armbands and around her neck she wore a golden torc. Her tunic and cloak were woven from the wool of multicoloured sheep. The two Roman blokes who wrote about Boudicca commented on her having a harsh voice but I don't believe that to be true. These men were obviously not used to women being the boss. For harshness read command-ing. I am woman, hear me roar! Boudicca knew how to fire up her troops. This leader would keep a live hare hidden about her person. At the end of a rousing call to battle she would lift up her garments and out the creature would appear. This long-eared animal then ran in a favoured direction thus signifying victory and good luck. In tribute to Boudicca I sometimes house a hamster in my bra.

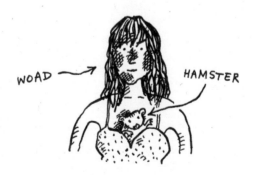

WOAD →   HAMSTER

---

* **R** In the last couple of seconds, Gyles, I've got you on repetition of the word 'second'.

† **R** I'm hoping here that 'size' and 'sighs' would catch a reader out by buzzing in on an incorrect challenge of repetition – worth a try.

HADRIAN'S WALL

Hadrian's Wall, or Adrian's Wail* as it was known in ancient times for the hardship it caused, is an early example of why challenging the might of a superpower invariably ends in tears. This is what happened to battered and bruised Rocky Balboa, celebrated for his anguished cries for girlfriend Adrianna Pennino, when he took on and almost defeated the undisputed world champion. True to his name, he was a son of the rugged border country of present-day Scotland. To the south lay the fat lands of Roman Britannia, which our fearless hero and his mates had long cast envious eyes on. Their constant raids and attacks led to the construction of a wall across the northern boundary of the province from Wallsend on the Tyne, 73 miles westwards to the Solway Firth. Soldiers began building work around AD 120 and for nearly 300 years it helped control troublesome neighbours from the north. But no barricade or heavily manned fortress could prevent RB from battling for his lifelong dream. One pummelling against the majesty of Apollo followed another and the memory of his ferocious onslaught is preserved today in Adrian's Wail.†

* Neat combining of the history of Roman Britain with the films of Sylvester Stallone, eh?

† **R** Repetition – but just as the whistle went! That's the way to do it.

SUTTON HOO

You may well ask hoo this person was. Speculation hinted at Ms S Stracke, real housewife of Beverly Hills and owner of the celebrated West Hollywood boutique that bears her name. Then along came Netflix and Ralph Fiennes to shed light (after digging up a great deal of soil) on the mystery. Their conclusion? Excavating in and around Cheam was a waste of time.* The answer lay in Carey Mulligan's back garden just outside Woodbridge in Suffolk. There, among untidy lumps and bumps that played havoc with her lawnmower, was where The Dig should be. First came an iron rivet. Then another. Dozens more followed as an Anglo-Saxon ship burial was unearthed and in it metalwork treasure dating from the early seventh century. This started a major rethink about what Britain might have been like in that era. But it still didn't answer the 'H' question. The smart money is on Rædwald, King of East Anglia, but we still don't know for sure.

* **D** Cheam is nowhere near Sutton Hoo and calls for a challenge for deviation. However, a defence could be mounted on the grounds that a deviation is valid in these circumstances. If you found yourself driving south in search of Sutton, when you should be heading northeast to Chelmsford (not Cheam) in the direction of Sutton Hoo, wouldn't you welcome a deviation? It's a moot point.

OFFA'S DYKE

The second half of the eighth century was a troubled time for the Kingdom of Mercia. Powerful King Offa had constantly to defend his lands from invasion and sometime during the 780s he decided that enough was – well, satisfactory.*† So, he called on the counsel of a wise man from Leicester recorded in history as Offa's D. Icke. As the self-styled 'Son of the Godhead' he knew all there was to know about alien conspiracies: a former goal-keeper at Oxford, Northampton and Hereford he had watched too many opponents' goal-bound shots whizz by into his net. So, his advice to the Mercian king was to move the posts, rip up the turf and build a mighty touchline to keep out marauding teams from Wales. Bands of workmen were organised to construct this mighty earthwork stretching nearly 180 miles from Liverpool Bay to the Severn Estuary. Originally, up to 20 metres wide and two thousand four hundred centimetres high in places, the legacy of Offa's Dyke is still visible in places to this day.

---

* **H** This highlights a classic example of hesitation arising from the sudden realisation that the repetition of 'enough' had to be avoided. However, a degree of academic scepticism does give legitimate pause for thought. Some scholars suggest that construction work on the 'dyke' began a couple of centuries before the reign of King Offa. Others rule him out altogether, making the point that in Old English the word *ofer* means an 'edge' or 'border'. Of course, the audience would have nodded off if this digression ever made it on to the airwaves.

† **R** On the subject of 'reduplicative phrases', the worst group to have in your mind during *Just A Minute* is … ABBA. As if 'Honey Honey', 'Ring Ring' and 'Andante Andante' weren't enough, there's 'Money Money Money' and, most dangerous of all, 'I Do I Do I Do I Do I Do'.

2

Norman Wisdom

THE VIKINGS ARE COMING

The Vikings were rough, hairy men from Scandinavia, who wore outlandish headgear and travelled the seven seas* in long ships (although no one knew how many large areas of saline water there were over a thousand years ago). The Vikings quickly became unwelcome visitors after a band of them pitched up on the beach at the Northumbrian monastery of Lindisfarne on 8 June 793. They weren't after absolution or a meaningful spiritual exchange on original sin. These marauders wanted plunder and slaughtered defenceless monks to get it. This was just the start. Jarrow, the Shetlands, the Hebrides and Orkneys were hit in the following 12 months. Twenty-four lunar-cycles later attacks began on Iona. At the mouth of the Rhine, Dorestad (the West's greatest trading centre) was targeted, too.† Alcuin of York sagely concluded it was God's punishment on the English for too much rumpy-pumpy. Historians point to a population boom in Scandinavia (excessive 'how's your Faeroe'?), leading to food shortages and the need to find sustenance and spoil elsewhere.

---

* Namely: the Indian Ocean, the Arctic and Antarctic big bodies of water, the North and South Atlantic H_2O extravagancies and the North and South Pacific dittos.

† **D** Deviation might seem an obvious challenge since the mouth of the Rhine is not in Britain. Such a challenge, though, would be ruled incorrect. This raises an important factor in playing and following the game: attention to the wording of the chosen topic. Although the subject in this instance is 'The Vikings Are Coming', it doesn't specify where they are coming from. Viking raiders didn't stop when they reached Britain. Much of western Europe suffered Viking attacks, from northwest Germany right down to Spain, and round into the Mediterranean all the way to Italy. Around the year 1000, Viking sailors even made it across the Atlantic to spend a winter in North America. So this should be classified as an incorrect challenge.

HOW ALFRED BURNT THE CAKES

He's come down through the ages as Alfred the Grate, first king of England and the originator of *The Great British Bake Off*. But, as Henry Ford opined, 'History is more or less bunk', so let's start with the cakes. The story of the Anglo-Saxon ruler who let a Somerset peasant woman's baking scorch in the fire didn't appear until a good couple of centuries after Alfred's death.* A bit of an afterthought, maybe? Calling yourself the first 'King of the English' was tricky back then too, given that country (as we know it) didn't exist. Alfred was King of Wessex and added the kingdom of Cornwall during his reign. But Aethelstan, Alfred's grandson, was the first true king† of a united land. But grandpa Alfred deserves his place in posterity for bringing an end to the Dark Ages when he invented a candle that kept the time and maintained the lights. He also defeated the Danes in several key battles and went into the newspaper business, starting the *Anglo-Saxon Chronicle*, which has been exasperating students ever since.

CAKES COOKED PERFECTLY...

CAKES OVERCOOKED BY TWO CENTURIES...

* **D** A couple of centuries is 'far, far too late' for a challenge to this deviation.

† **R** Three unnecessary repetitions of 'king' there. After the first use, alternatives such as monarch and sovereign should have been used.

THE TRUTH ABOUT ETHELRED THE UNREADY

This rather depends on how you look at his reign. When it comes to producing heirs and spares, among Anglo-Saxon kings Ethelred runs a very close second to Edward the Elder, who sired 18 legitimate offspring to Ethelred's 16. So, from poor Mrs Etheldred's point of view, her old man was 'ready' and up for it much of the time. On the other hand, it could be argued that conceiving such a sizeable royal brood might have taken his mind off the job in hand – ruling, you understand. That being the case, it's understandable that history remembers Ethelred the Unready as a rather ineffectual monarch who couldn't stop the Danes overrunning England during his two spells on the throne from 978 to 1016. The major snag is that Ethelred wasn't 'unready' at all. He was 'Unraed', an Old English word which means 'no counsel', or 'poorly advised'. To add insult to injury, it was also a pun on the king's name: Ethelred also has a meaning in the language of *Beowulf* – ironically, 'noble advisor'.*

* R A knowledge of the history of the English language can be useful here. In the case highlighted above, repetition of the term Anglo-Saxon has been circumvented by referring to *Beowulf*, the most celebrated work written in that language.

EDMUND IRONSIDE AND KING CANUTE

This pair were quite a double act. Edmund raised one army after another to repel the Danes, Canute tried to turn back the tide and they both managed to be King of England in the same year – 1016; although poor old Edmund only played the gig for 221 days before being hooked off. There are suspicions that Canute may have had a hand in his rival's demise: on the anniversary of Edmund's death, he visited his grave and draped it with a peacock-decorated cloak to help Edmund into the afterlife, the bird in question symbolising resurrection. Canute was also a killjoy. In addition to trying to put an end to the seaside fun of building sandcastles to defy the incoming sea, he took a dim view of the rather relaxed Anglo-Saxon attitude to that other popular holiday pastime: a bit of how's your father. Under Canute's law, a woman found guilty of adultery forfeited her property to her husband and had her ears and nose cut off for good measure. It didn't last.

LADY GODIVA

Unwrapped and exposed, the temptingly delicious Lady Godiva embodied sensual luxury, taste and class – which must have been a tough call as the eleventh-century wife of Earl Leofric of Mercia. The hair-extension business owes his spouse a big thank you too; although makers of door viewers haven't had a good word for the countess for the best part of 1000 years. The unrobed equestrian legend stems from the lady's husband's measures to sort out the traffic in Coventry. As a final resort, Leo* turned to big taxis. The people objected majorly. Godiva sympathised and made repeated efforts to persuade him to change his mind. Probably hoping to close the matter for good, he agreed to get rid of them if she pioneered a different mode of transport: riding on horseback through the streets, stark naked. Godiva did as requested, with just her flowing locks to preserve her modesty. All the people stayed inside. The streets were empty and the only victim that day was Peeping Tom, who enjoyed himself too much doing what he shouldn't have and went blind.

* **R** Nice play, using Leo as an acceptable variant of Leofric, thereby avoiding repetition.

THE BAYEUX TAPESTRY

Let's get something straightened out from the off. The Bayeux Tapestry isn't a tapestry at all; it's an embroidery – all 68.3 metres of it.* It's also a huge contradiction, marking a famous first and celebrated last. As a kind of comic-book account of the Norman Conquest, it depicts the sole successful French invasion of England (apparently it inspired Napoleon to have another try getting on for 750 years later, and we know what became of that). The 'tapestry' also records the final successful occupation of Great Britain by enemy forces and it does so in painstaking detail. You might spare a thought for poor Mrs Conqueror (aka Queen Matilda) and her chums, stitching and bitching for months on end – only the official record is probably leading you astray here, so you can hold back on the pity. As a piece of propaganda (isn't history always written by victors?), it was probably commissioned by Odo, half-brother to the new king, who wanted it for his recently finished cathedral at Bayeux, where it remained largely unknown for several centuries.†

---

* ◳ Another successful technique is to appear to cast doubt on the topic. This distracts other contestants while they mentally change track, buys time and uses up seconds.

† Nowadays, it would of course be posted as a series of woven images on Twitter, headed 'read the whole thread'.

GREAT NORMANS

Norman Foster, Norman Hartnell, Norman Mailer, Norman Parkinson,* Stormin' Norman, Fatboy Slim – there have been famous Normans throughout our history, but the greatest of them all wasn't called Norman at all. He was named William the Conqueror – except he wasn't. Never mind 1066 and all that, there was no one with that name in Normandy in the early eleventh century because the nomenclature didn't exist. And why? 'W' did not exist in the Norman French alphabet. 'Ah, ha!' I hear you say, 'what about the appearance of that very letter on the celebrated embroidery (see page 25) recording his conquest of England?' This, you may be interested to know, is an early example of the melding of the language spoken by the occupiers with that of their now vanquished subjects. The commander of the victorious force was known as Guillaume by his followers, who would have written it in Latin as Guillelemus. The closest his newly defeated vassals could get to that was the Germanic: Wilhelm, and its English equivalent, the appellation by which the first Norman king has become known.

---

* ℝ *Anaphora* is a literary device with two opposing uses that can crop up regularly. Here it's deployed as a rhetorical gambit where the same word is repeated at the beginning of each phrase to add emphasis – in this instance to the name 'Norman'. As a grammatical tool, however, anaphora avoids repetition; a frequently cited example being the statement, 'I like it and so do they', where anaphora is used to avoid repeating the words 'like' and 'it', where the sentence might be rendered, 'I like it and they like it as well.'

THE DOMESDAY BOOK

If you want a bureaucratic cock-up, look no further than the Domesday Book. OK – it was a rush job. William the Conqueror (aka William the Bastard – actually he was illegitimate, as well as being a right sod to the English) must have been a bit slow out on the uptake, because it took him nearly 20 years to twig that not all his subjects were paying their fair share of taxes. So he sent inspectors throughout the realm meticulously recording who owned what and where. (Note the pronoun; it's important.) They accomplished this so thoroughly that, according to one contemporary historian, 'there was no single hide nor indeed was one ox or cow or pig left out that was not put down in this record.' And, this was completed at breakneck speed in the eight months to August 1086. Brilliant – except for one tiny detail: the word mentioned above. Back then, most folk in England didn't have surnames. The king had all the data he needed to boost his revenue, but he didn't know how to identify people correctly to make them cough up. And that's why we have family names to follow those we're christened with.

THE MURDER OF THOMAS BECKET

The murder of Thomas Becket robbed the early medieval period of one its greatest players on the national stage. His now celebrated drama *Waiting for Godot* may have bombed in London, but he did a swift ID swap and soon found success as Samuel Beckett. Becket was as much at home among les Français as he was in Angleterre. Channel hopping in his own ships, he amassed a fortune, became a close friend of royalty (he and Henry II were great pals for a while) and, like other writers who needed day work to cover thin patches in the writing game, he got himself a couple of plum jobs: first Chancellor of England and then Archbishop of Canterbury.* But the latter put a big strain on Becket's relationship with the king, who decided he was getting far too big for his boots; when Becket returned from France to play the 1170 Christmas season, he was welcomed by cheering crowds. The monarch blew his top and four of his hangers-on decided to end Becket's run. Of course, this backfired and killing off Becket has only made his work more popular ever since.

---

* **D** A challenger might question what this has to do with Becket's murder. But a legitimate defence can be offered since it was Thomas Becket's acquisition of power and influence that brought about his downfall. As for the other writers alluded to, you can take your pick from the likes of Geoffrey Chaucer (a customs chief in London) or Samuel Pepys (who earned his crust running the navy. Pepys was also an MP.) But should anyone challenge it, this literary diversion certainly amounts to deviation.

THE FIRST EISTEDDFOD*†

Tune your harps! Loosen the vocal cords! Don your bedsheets! Let's hear it for the Eisteddfod, that centuries-old landmark on the cultural scene of Wales. The first was held in 1176, when Lord Rhys decided to brighten things up now that the Dark Ages were long past. He sent messengers across the land to invite poets and musicians from all over to get together in his castle in Cardigan for a festival of song and verse – an early medieval Glastonbury with less mud, no hipsters and none of the ghastly traffic jams that bring the west of England to a standstill. Eisteddfods have been pulling in crowds ever since – fans eager to see their idols walk off with one of the two chairs given as prizes every year. The Eisteddfod has it all. A lot of rallies are held in Wales – the motor ones, not the political – and crowds of petrolheads pack out every performance of Bizet's ever-popular *Car Men*. At the last Eisteddfod I attended, the highlight was a performance of *Dai Fledermaus*, an opera all about Batman moving from Gotham City to Swansea.

---

* Different Welsh words offer different 'deviation' perils for the non-Welsh speaker trying to say them. 'Eisteddfod' is relatively safe; spinach you need to be brave with (*sbigoglys*) and if you're lucky enough to be able to navigate its 18 syllables, that Anglesey place name could take up an entire minute: Llanfairpwll …

† … gwyngyllgogerychwyrndrobwllllantysiliogogogoch.

HUMAN HISTORY SO FAR

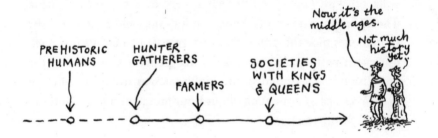

3

Kings and Queens

THE KINGS AND QUEENS OF ENGLAND

For a start I can tell you their names, starting with the king known as the Conqueror, because there was a little poem listing them that I learnt at school. If I remember the verse completely correctly, I may get challenged, so I'm going to tread carefully. Here goes. Wish me luck.

William, Willie, Harry, Steve the turd;*
Hal, Dick, John, Henry Third;
Edward One, Two, Three, Rick again;
Henrys Four, Five, Six, and then?
Eds Fourth and Fifth, Richard the Bad,
Harrys twain and Ned the lad.
Mary, Lizzie, James the Vain;
Charlie, Charles, plus Jim again.
Bill and Mary, Anne o' Gloria;
a quartet of Georges, Will, I , V, and Victoria.
Eddie Number Seven, George half-of-ten,
Eduardo briefly, Bro Geo and Lilibet not yet in heaven.
And after her it's Chas and Wills,
and to complete my royal-naming orgy
along should come a sixth king called Georgie.

---

* **D** Instances like this, where historical conjectures arise, can lead to challenges for deviation. A challenger might propose the thesis that King Stephen was a good guy and therefore question this departure from the historical record. Recollections may vary, though.

FINE DINING A THOUSAND YEARS AGO

You needed a strong stomach for 'fine dining' back then. 'I am a binder and scourger and soon become a thrower. Sometimes I cast an old fellow to the ground.' That's a contemporary riddle describing a popular drink. Any guesses what it was? Not wine, which in Anglo-Saxon times was light and fruity, and less than 4 per cent proof. Pah! Beer, or *beor*,* didn't have much of a kick either, and it had the consistency and taste of over-sugared porridge. No, for serious boozing a millennium ago, you had to get stuck into mead: the super-sweet, heady brew made from crushed honeycombs. By our standards the delicacies it washed down posed challenges of their own. The burbot, or eel-pout and no more attractive than its name suggests, was an uninviting, wriggly offering. Even less appealing, with its large sucker-like mouth, was the lamprey. But, boy, did our forebears like them! In fact, William the Conqueror's youngest son, Henry I, went to meet his Maker in 1135 after scoffing 'a surfeit' of you know what. Don't say I didn't warn you.

A SURFEIT OF LAMPREYS

Even ONE lamprey is a surfeit, Henry.

I'll have yours. I LOVE 'em.

Twenty lampreys a day keeps the doctor away...

---

* This trick needs to be used sparingly. You could try 'didn't have, or hæbban, much of a kick, or kike, either, or *oeghweðer* ...' but would rapidly be reminded of the unwritten *Just A Minute* rule about not being an *ærs*.

GOING TO UNI A
THOUSAND YEARS AGO

The truth is that no one went to uni in Britain a thousand years ago, because there were no universities. That at least, is what present-day historians tell us. Look back in the past, however, and the story changes. It's generally accepted that the first British institution of tertiary education came into being in a market town beside a livestock crossing on the River Thames. The place was called Oxford, but when it began to shake its academic plumage is open conjecture. The *Historiola* of 1375 credits exiles from the Trojan War with getting the seat of learning going. Writing in 1490, John Rous places its origin in biblical times, thanks to the otherwise wicked King Mempricius. Three centuries later, John Ayliffe pushes its foundation on to 'the year of our Lord eight hundred and eighty-six', which is where Alfred the Great gets a look-in according to some accounts. Modern history (and in my student days that started in 1066!) records teaching at my *alma mater* as early as three decades later. Not quite a millennium but getting closer.*

---

* Here's another example of the importance of paying attention to the precise wording of the subject title. The piece delivered is undeniably lucid, interesting and avoids the three pitfalls that give rise to challenges. However, the topic is 'Going to uni a thousand years ago' and the whole piece focuses on why *no one could go* to uni a thousand years ago.

MAGNA CARTA

Magna Carta isn't packed with laughs, but here's something to raise a smile. A tour bus grinds slowly through congested London streets before reaching the suburbs and eventually pulling up at a meadow beside the River Thames in Surrey. 'This is Runnymede, where Magna Carta was signed,' says the guide. 'When was that?' asks one of the tourists. 'Twelve fifteen,' comes the reply. 'Damn, traffic,' mutters the disgruntled questioner. 'Missed it by forty minutes.' It's not the joke's fault. The whole matter of Magna Carta is riddled with inaccuracies. First up is the name. The historic document is actually called *Magna Carta Libertatum* (the Great Charter of Liberties to you and me) and it didn't acquire this until several years after the year one thousand two hundred and ten plus five. Then there's the matter of its authorisation. No one put their signature on Magna Carta.* King John gave his OK with the royal seal, but this wasn't something he did in person; officials saw to that on his behalf. Besides which, the man on the throne wouldn't have minded if he had missed the event altogether, because Magna Carta legally restricted the power of the monarch, in favour of the Church and powerful barons. Oh, yes, the rights of the common people also got a mention, but they were a long way down the pecking order.

---

* As there's no definite article in the document's name, you need only use the phrase 'signed the Magna Carta' if you want to make a pedant's blood boil.

WHAT I KNOW ABOUT EDWARD LONGSHANKS

The elder son of Henry III was known by a couple of nicknames. The 'Longshanks' bit was down to his stature. Standing over six feet he was a one of the tallest kings in English history and siring 19 legitimate offspring might suggest physical prowess elsewhere. Edward's antipathy to the people of Scotland led to regular bust-ups north of the border – he was buried with the Latin inscription *Scotorum malleus* – 'Hammer of the Scots' – as Mel Gibson's grisly end in *Braveheart* makes clear. Longshanks didn't have many friends in Wales either, despite boosting Welsh tourism by building romantic medieval castles around the country. He gave politicians short shrift. His reign saw the shortest parliament in our British story, which lasted just one day: 30 May 1306. However, he did have a softer side. After the death of Eleanor of Castile, his much-loved child-bride (she was barely 12 when they married, he was 15), he had crosses erected at the places where her funeral cortège halted, the last of them at the eponymous Charing site, in London.

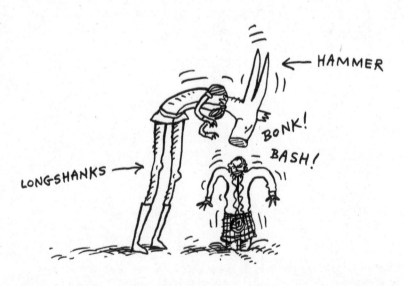

THE STONE OF SCONE

The Stone of Scone has been part of Scottish coronation razz-matazz for centuries, when successive rulers marked their reign as champion with a rock cake.* So English kings didn't have it all their own way in the Great British Bake Off. Even though its texture and taste were nothing to write home about, greedy Edward I still wanted his slice. In 1296, he took the Stone of Scone as spoils of war and fitted it into the chair in Westminster Abbey on which most subsequent sovereigns have been crowned. Roll forward to Christmas morning 1950 and the half-baked scheme of four Caledonian students to turn up the heat of history, nick the Stone of Scone and spirit it back north of the border – managing to break it in two in the process! Their heist crumbled and within four months the stone was returned Westminster, where it stayed until the 700th anniversary of Longshanks's 'acquisition', when the government sent it to be kept in Edinburgh Castle, until the next monarch is crowned.

STONE   SCONE

<hr />

* Nice use of the pun Scone (the ancient capital of Scotland in Perthshire) and scone (the small cake made from flour, fat and milk) – although the pronunciation of the vowel in the latter varies: rhyming with either 'gone' or 'throne'.

THE FIRST PRINCE OF WALES

It is a time-honoured tradition that the British monarch's eldest son is always the Prince of Wales, a hereditary institution that dates back to 1284, when Edward I (Longshanks again) presented his first, newborn, male child to the Welsh chieftains at Caernarvon Castle as Prince of Wales. Right? Wrong! The king's baby boy was in fact his fourth of that sex, whose elder brother (with the very English name Alfonso!) was still alive and well. Furthermore, Prince Edward had to wait until he was 17 before being given the title and even then his 'creation' took place at Lincoln, over 180 miles from the legendary setting. Not that the leaders of Cymru got a look-in there either – they had to troop off to Chester to pay their homage to their new prince. His only historic connection with the royal town in Gwynedd is that he was born there. Of course, he wasn't the first Prince of Wales at all. A string of rulers with genuine native pedigrees had claimed that nifty and noble nomenclature before him, the first of whom was Dafydd ap Llywelyn four decades earlier.

ROBERT THE BRUCE AND HIS SPIDER

The great Robert the Bruce – and the spider that inspired him to lead his nation to victory – live on to this day in Scottish folklore. Just watch rugby internationals against the Auld Enemy to see why. You can picture the scene (or if you can't, find it on YouTube). Murrayfield is packed to capacity. Out on the hallowed turf, the opposing teams stand proudly awaiting the national anthems.* First comes the somewhat grudging rendition of 'God Save the Queen'. Then the moment arrives: the skirl of the pipes and the stadium erupts as tens of thousands of Scotsmen burst into song:

> *O Flower of Scotland*
> *When will we see your like again*
> *That fought and died for*
> *Your wee bit hill and glen.*
> *And stood against him,*
> *Proud Edward's army,*
> *Then sent him homeward*
> *Tae think again.*

And it's all down to the spider – or so legend would have it. Written to commemorate Bruce's celebrated triumph over a far larger English force at Bannockburn in 1314, this unofficial national anthem celebrates the king's perseverance after repeated military setbacks, when a spider trying repeatedly to build its web until it succeeded encouraged him to keep bashing – not unlike the national rugger team at times, so I'm told.

---

* **D** This is an interesting one. One could claim that holding forth about international rugby matches between Scotland and England has nothing to do with either Robert the Bruce or his spider. But one might also legitimately claim that Scotsmen taking to the field to do battle against rampaging Englishmen is precisely what this topic is all about.

ROBIN HOOD

Robin Hood, Robin Hood, riding through the glen
Robin Hood, Robin Hood, with his band of men
Feared by the bad, loved by the good
*Robin Hood, Robin Hood, Robin Hood.**

For four years, beginning in 1955, episodes of *The Adventures of Robin Hood* opened once a week on ITV with this stirring song. What most of us watching at the time didn't know was that the outlaw of the legend was as much figment of popular imagination as the television character played by Richard Greene. Was there ever a Robin Hood? And, if there was, which was he, because folklore has thrown up many claimants to the name? The earliest reference dates from William Langland's *Piers Plowman*, penned around 1377. That's a couple of centuries after one of the front-runners was rebelling against Henry II. This chap was named David, Earl of Huntingdon, whose wife was called Matilda. Come the sixteenth century, and in a play written by Anthony Munday, Dave has transmogrified into Robert and his squeeze into Marion. Other theories identify Robin Hood as a Yorkshireman. One even suggests this time-honoured English hero was a Scotsman! Let's move swiftly on the noo.

---

* **R** We've had anaphora before, and this is another classic example.

JOAN OF ARC AND
THE HUNDRED YEARS WAR

As historical dramas go, the Hundred Years War was desperately slooooooow – it actually lasted 116 years until 1453, but no one had the heart to let on it was running way over time. The Irish playwright George Bernard Shaw used it for his 1923 play *Saint Joan*, but even he was so uncertain of the reception of this Eurocentric tussle between us and the French that he opened the piece on Broadway rather than in London. The highpoint for many observers was the brief trouser-role cameo by a teenage ingénue who stole the show courtesy of some theatrical angels. They gave her the confidence to convince the king to let her lead an army against the English forces besieging the city of Orléans. Quite honestly, Charles VII didn't have a lot to lose. Why not kit out this Joan girl in armour and see what the troops made of her? She went down a storm. The siege was lifted. Home victories followed until Calais was England's only possession across the Channel. But by then poor Joan had made her final exit: burned at the stake – for wearing men's clothes, among other trumped-up charges.

MEDIEVAL TIMELINE OF LIFE EXPECTANCY

WELL $\longrightarrow$ UNWELL OR INJURED $\longrightarrow$ DEAD

ooooooh...

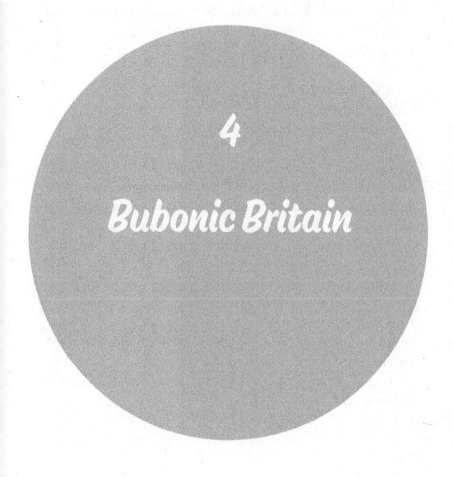

4

Bubonic Britain

THE BLACK DEATH

The Black Death? It sounds like a heavy metal band? Or a Guinness-based hangover cure that goes terribly wrong? West End business during lockdown? Maybe New Zealand's epic 19–7 loss to England in the 2019 Rugby World Cup semi-final? Nope. It's a nursery rhyme:

> *Ring-a-ring o' roses,*
> *A pocket full of posies,*
> *A-tishoo! The same sound again!**
> *We all fall down.*

How so? Red blotches on the skin, sweet-smelling flowers to ward off infection, the sneezing fits of victims of pneumonic plague and dropping down dead – to quote the TV insurance ad: 'Simples.' Except that it isn't. The ditty didn't appear in print until 1881 and versions sung in other countries made no reference to horrid pathogens, never mind *Yersinia pestis*. Then there are the symptoms alluded to. They're nothing like the ghastly black swellings that come with what our forebears called 'a touch of the bubonics'. No, the whole jingle thing is a joke – unlike the Black Death of the second half of the fourteenth century, which killed 30 to 60 per cent of the population of Europe and was most likely spread by human fleas, nor those of much-maligned rats.

---

* **R** Elegant variation, substitution of a word or phrase with another to avoid repetition, is a vital arrow in the quiver of anyone playing *Just A Minute* with an eye on the target and an ear for the blast on the whistle indicating that they have scored a hit. So is *pleonasm*, as demonstrated above: the use of more words than are necessary to convey meaning. A simpler example of pleonasm might be the expression 'see with one's own eyes', where 'see' would suffice.

MEDICINE IN THE MIDDLE AGES

Take my advice. If you're ever moved to travel back in time don't get ill during the Middle Ages – no, seriously, avoid it. If the pandemic described on page 303 isn't warning enough, consider the following. They didn't know about blood circulation in the Middle Ages, so no one checked your pulse for signs of life. Instead, they put a bowl of water on your chest to see if you were breathing. Got an infectious disease? More often than not, you'd be tucked up in bed with another victim because the idea of spreading germs hadn't dawned on anyone. Then there was God. Sickness and disease was the means He used to test the faith of the afflicted. Snuff it and your belief in the Almighty wasn't up to scratch; survive and it was. Planetary misalignments were blamed for all manner of medical disasters, too. The conjunction of Saturn and Jupiter in 1348–9 caused 'the pernicious corruption of the surrounding air, as well as a sign of mortality, famine and other catastrophes', which we know as the Black Death.

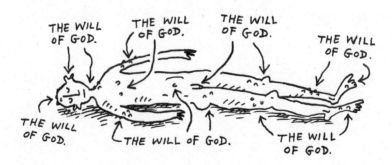

PHYSICIAN'S CHART FROM THE MIDDLE AGES SHOWING FATAL ILLNESSES:

THE WILL OF GOD.

THE WILL OF GOD.

THE WILL OF GOD.

THE WILL OF GOD.

THE WILL OF GOD.

THE WILL OF GOD.

THE WILL OF GOD.

CHESS

If you think you know chess – the 'Queen's Gambit' and the rest – think again if you were playing in the Middle Ages. It was a very different game in those days. The king's consort (known as the 'prime minister' back then) was only able to move one square in each direction. Just to add to the fun (aka 'confusion'), bishops (called 'elephants') could move just two places along diagonals, although they were allowed to jump over others on the board. But this set of moves was part of the steady evolution of a playful contest that had been around since before the six hundreds, when written accounts began in the Middle East, where chess flourished having arrived from India several centuries earlier. Tim Rice and ABBA got in on the act in the mid-1980s. Harry Potter and chums enjoy wizard chess in which pieces communicate with the players. The first chess match between a human and a machine took place in 2001 (according to Kubrick's *Space Odyssey* of that date). While, 16 years later, Homer Simpson morphed into a chess savant in an episode of his eponymous show. No wonder Netflix couldn't resist leaping on the bandwagon with their hit series referenced above.

THE PEASANTS' REVOLT

The Peasants' Revolt was started by the Poll Tax. Not the one that heralded Margaret Thatcher's downfall. They named hers the Community Charge because the levy* we're talking about here still carried mutinous overtones over 600 years later. Richard II was on the throne, working on his legacy for Shakespeare's play about him and attending to his personal hygiene. Next time you use a hankie, spare him a thought because he's credited with introducing it into Britain. Whenever you fasten the loo door, thank this unhappy monarch too for individual WCs; until he promoted them, doing your personal business was a communal affair. The king's problem was that the peasants weren't that fussed about wiping their noses, or anywhere else in private.† They wanted to be freed from serfdom and heavy taxation – and in 1381 they had leverage. The Black Death had caused widespread labour shortages and people were demanding higher wages. The revolt started in Essex and ended in London, where the leader was killed and the 14-year-old ruler largely agreed to the rebels' demands, boosting British democracy.

---

* **R** Another example of 'elegant variation' and a chance to note that when this phrase was coined, 'elegant' may have meant 'annoyingly fussy': certainly, watching someone dance around trying to avoid the repetition of a word can be excruciating … outside of *Just A Minute*.

† **D** This diversion into the personal habits of King Richard II strays close to being challenged for deviation. However, it manages to maintain interest in the topic, thereby distracting potential challengers, before smartly reverting to the phrasing in the subject title through heavy emphasis on the word 'peasants', helped by the clever use of alliteration that links it with 'problem' four words earlier.

THE WIFE OF BATH

The Wife of Bath? That rather depends on who you're talking about. Alexander George Thynn, 7th Marquess of Bath, had one official wife, but there were several dozen 'wifelets', with quite a few dotted around his Longleat estate. On the other hand, Geoffrey Chaucer's Wife of Bath notched up five husbands and was keen to nab a sixth. Although the pair of them were over 600 years apart, they had more than a name in common.* They shared a vigorous enjoyment of good old rumpy-pumpy and both took delight in cocking a snook at the social norms of their day. Where tabloid readers were riveted by accounts of Lord Bath's carryings on, most people picking up a newly published copy of *The Canterbury Tales* at the end of the fourteenth century would have been scandalised by Geoff C's good lady's opinions on marriage and the battle of the sexes. What women most desired, she contended, was control of husbands, lives and households. Was she an early feminist icon? You could say so … and many do.

WIFE OF BATH   HUSBANDS OF BATH

---

* Clever blending of two distinctive characters from both sides of the eternal matrix of male/female relationship, especially when they're separated by well over half a millennium of history.

THE BATTLE OF AGINCOURT

Henry V's great victory at the Battle of Agincourt in 1415 marked a particularly low point for the French, or *Les Français* as they like to refer to themselves. Not only was their much superior army beaten by a far smaller English force, but it also heralded the arrival of a new language, developed with naughty pleasure on our side of the Channel. This was a cod version of their mode of communication called franglais. Shakespeare chips in when the victor in his eponymous play mangles her native tongue trying to woo Princess Katherine. Later, Kenneth Williams entered the lists with his own endearing love ditty, sung to the tune of 'Auld Lang Syne', which began:

> *Honi soi qui mal y pense*
> *Faits vos jeux, reconnaissance*
> *Hammersmith Palais de danses*
> *Badinage, ma crêpe Suzette.*

To celebrate the Battle of Agincourt, here's my variation on this classic verse:

> *Corsage, massage, triage, brioche,*
> *Pain au chocolat, à la carte, Juliette Binoche.*
> *Baguette, banquette, vinaigrette,*
> *Quelle horreur, agent provocateur, brunette,*
>
> *Au pair, pas de deux, tête-à-tête*
> *Bataille d'Agincourt – c'est chouette!*
> *Faux pas, Grand Prix, espionage,*
> *Gruyère, Camembert, fromage,*
> *Mayonnaise, Nigel Farage,*
> *RSVP, Battle of Agincourt!*

Vive le Lime Cordial!

---

* **D** Sharp-eared students of legitimate and illegitimate French may well spot that the examples quoted are less true franglais and more a confection of random French words loosely strung together for entertainment rather than elucidation.

THE FIRST MISPRINT

The first misprint was made right at the start of British printing and typesetters have been at it ever since. The story begins in the fifteenth century with the claim that the first repeated production of books took place in Oxford, under Alsatian maestro Wynkyn de Worde, and not in London, where William Caxton plied his trade. The evidence for this was based on the catchily titled *Expositio in Symbolum Apostolorum* and its '1468' Oxonian imprint which, if correct, would have hit the bookshops* several years ahead of Mr C's earliest examples. (At the end of the seventeenth century, court cases raging over who had the right to manufacture reading material cited this as proof of their claim.) Unfortunately, all the brouhaha was based on a simple typo: the date on the hardback from the city of dreaming spires should have read one thousand four hundred and seventy-eight, a year after printer Bill first created a tome in this manner in England.†

---

* **R** Elegant variation is put to good use again in this entry, where it is employed to skirt round the pitfall of repeating the words 'printing' and 'books'. However, some might argue that 'book' is in fact repeated in 'bookshops'. This raises an interesting philosophical question and one much enjoyed by bibliophiles. Is 'bookshops' in fact a repetition of the word 'book'? To analyse this further requires evaluation of the two nouns. What is a book? A bound volume of printed pages (either casebound, or softbound). So far, so good. And 'bookshops'? These are retail premises in which a book or books are offered for sale. Therefore, we can deduce that a book is an article that one can buy, and bookshops are places where one may purchase them. By this analysis 'book' and 'bookshops' are nouns referring to two quite distinct and separate entities that happen to be linked through a commercial transaction. On this basis, the use of 'bookshops' (above) does not constitute a repetition of 'book' (also above).

† **D** The misprint is, perhaps, the written word's first example of deviation – especially those that appeared in such holy books as 'The Judas Bible' (where Judas's name appears instead of Jesus's) and 'The Wicked Bible' (where a missing 'not' leaves the unfortunate commandment 'Thou shalt commit adultery').

DANCING ROUND THE MAYPOLE

It was Sir Arnold Bax, the underrated English composer, who said, 'In this life you should try everything once, except for incest and folk dancing.' So, dancing round the maypole held few delights for this maestro of the podium.* Seventeenth-century Puritans agreed and killed off one of great springtime rituals of medieval life. Moving clockwise, revellers held hands and danced, stamped and acted a set of ancient May rituals, following the melody of 'Here We Go Round the Mulberry Bush':

> *Let's circumvent the merry Maypole*
> *The joyous Maypole, the gladsome Maypole,*
> *Circle about the entertaining Maypole*
> *On a cold and frosty morning!*[†]

Maypoles were, of course, unashamedly phallic symbols – and some of them were truly enormous. Top billing probably goes to the one erected on the Strand in 1661, which stood 143 feet high. It might still be there (no doubt gumming up the traffic), if Sir Isaac Newton hadn't chopped it down to use as a support for Christiaan Huygens's equally massive reflecting telescope.

---

* By the way, how many maypole dancers does it take to change a light bulb? Five! Six! Seven! Eight!

† **R** Elegant variation again. Except for the limp choice of the fourth adjective before 'Maypole', one might never guess that 'entertaining', 'joyous' and 'gladsome' have been substituted for the adjective 'merry', which would otherwise appear in all four lines of the rhyme and therefore be repeated three times leading, no doubt, to a successful challenge.

THE WARS OF THE ROSES

The Wars of the Roses were fought in medieval England between an army of Yorkshiremen and another from across the county boundary in Lancashire. But they found their way to Hollywood, where its founding father liked to cram his films with superfluous detail,* to the point where Nicholas Bentley composed the clerihew:

> Cecil B. DeMille
> *Rather against his will*
> *Was persuaded to leave Moses*
> *Out of the Wars of the Roses.*

However, the movie parallel is not entirely misplaced. When the popular RSC trilogy *The Wars of the Roses* was revived in 2015, it was described as 'the first box set' – like *The Godfather* with chainmail. Shakespeare kicked off with *Henry VI*. Success demanded a sequel: the second part of the above play. Now on a winning run, he followed up with number three.† By way of a finale, the series concluded with *Richard the Third*, whose defeat and death at the field known as B-O-S-W-O-R-T-H brought the actual Lancastrian–Yorkist conflict to an end. And, should you need help remembering the other mêlées, try this mnemonic: '*A boy now will mention all the hot, horrid battles till Bosworth.*'‡ In longhand, they are: St Albans, Blore Heath, Northampton, Wakefield, Mortimer's Cross, the Second Battle of that Hertfordshire town just mentioned, Towton, Hedgy Moor, Hexham, Barnet, Tewkesbury and the B place.

---

* **D** Very subtle toying with the reader in this flirtation with a digression to Hollywood. By the time the penny drops and a finger is poised to protest, the discussion niftily slips back on message and returns to the specified topic.

† **R** A neat bit of *circumlocution* (the use of more words than necessary) was called for when discussing these early history plays. Shakespeare wrote three parts to *King Henry VI*, which lays a repetition trap for the unwary.

‡ Mnemonics are your friend, as they ease the reeling-off of merrily time-consuming lists. This is an especially good one, as it untangles the ambiguity of which 'b' is Barnet and which is Bosworth by including the word 'Bosworth' itself. If you fear you might still wonder where 'Blore Heath' comes, you can switch out 'boy' for a near-rhyme of 'Blore': 'A bore will now mention …'

THE PRINCES IN THE TOWER

Ah yes, the Princess in the Tower* – murdered, they say, at the command of Richard the Third. The great Sir Laurence Olivier portrayed the hunchback sovereign as a melodramatic baddie. Then the monarch's skeleton was dug up in Leicester in 2012, proving he was as physically unprepossessing as the legends had it. But the disappearance of the princess in the Tower is remembered as his darkest deed. It began with her loud-mouth father's boasts that she could spin straw into gold, which led to the incarceration of the maiden with a spinning-wheel, a pile of dried grain stalks and a royal warning that she was for the chop if she didn't turn it into the precious metal by the following day. This she managed to do, thanks to an ugly cove with a ridiculously contrived name no one could get right. But this didn't go well. He spun the treasure. The sovereign wanted more. The 'spinner' also wanted extra and the girl finally agreed to give him her first-born child. She married the king, became a royal and had a baby. She would have lost this too, if she hadn't stumbled across the appellation Rumpelstiltskin after drawing a blank with others like Richard Hunchback. The End – Nothing more was heard of the princess in the tower.

Of course I'm only a fictional character.

Me too.

***

* 🄷 Ingenious use of auditory avoidance – pretending to hear 'princess' instead of 'princes' – therefore side-stepping the need to speak about the disappearance of the surviving sons of Edward IV (the deposed Edward V aged twelve, and his nine-year-old brother, Richard of Shrewsbury, Duke of York) in the Tower of London in 1483, which could have led to hesitation if you're struggling to remember who they were, never mind what they were called.

5

Tudor Times

PERKIN WARBECK

We have a lot of time for the Perkins of this world, but this Warbeck bloke's identity crisis has to be one of British history's biggest disasters. For the record – that's to say after he was imprisoned and was being given the Tudor third degree – PW claimed to be a Flemish-born ex-pat who'd washed up in Ireland. So what? His problems began in 1490 when he maintained he was actually Richard of Shrewsbury, one of the princes who'd disappeared in the Tower of London a decade earlier. This would have made him the rightful heir to the throne of England and a direct challenger to King Henry VII. Some people got so carried away they began calling him Richard IV, which went to his head. He tried to land an invading army at Deal, but never made it off the boat.* Marching from Scotland didn't go much better. His last attempt started in Cornwall and ended in Hampshire. He escaped twice, despite considerable freedom at the royal court, and was hanged – a pretender to the last.

---

* **R** Forbidden witticism: So it was not Deal, but No Deal.

HENRY VIII

I'm 'Enery the Eighth, certainly,
'Enery the Eighth, that's me!
I got married to the widow next door,
She's been hitched seven times before
And every one was an 'Enery
She wouldn't have a Willie nor a Sam
I'm her eighth old man named 'Enery
'Enery the Eighth, to be sure!*

This was Harry Champion's signature song (with appropriate adjustments), which he sang in music halls up and down the country in the early 1900s. Joe Brown did well with his early sixties cover; George Harrison was a particular fan. But it was Herman's Hermits' release four years later that made the serious money, becoming the fastest selling single to that point, knocking '(I Can't Get No) Satisfaction' off the *Billboard* Hot 100 chart along the way. Purists may bridle at the liberties taken with British history. King Henry VIII† was a chap, of course. He had six spouses, not seven (though see page 61). And the previously married woman he wed had been the wife of just one previous husband: Henry's brother, Prince Arthur.

---

* **R** As many readers may know, the correct version of this song relies on the repetition of the phrases 'I'm' or 'I am', and the word 'married'. To avoid repetition, this doctored version has had to deploy quick-witted substitutes such as 'that's me' and 'hitched'.

† **D** Perhaps the best example of a fact which would count as a deviation but would be cruel not to share is the early controversy over the regnal name 'Elizabeth II'. Unlike England, Scotland had had no 'Elizabeth I' and the folk songs 'Sky High Joe' and 'The Ballad of the Inch' celebrate the popular practice of blowing up post boxes displaying the provocative letters 'ER II'.

UTOPIA

Utopia is the title of a notable work of fiction written in Latin by the great Sir Thomas More. Paul Scofield portrayed him as magisterial in the 1966 movie *A Man for All Seasons*. Just under 50 years later, in Anton Lesser's characterisation in *Wolf Hall*, he came across as pinched and pedantic. Neither played the author of *Utopia* for laughs. But he must have had a lighter side. After all, we're talking about the only saint to sit as an MP. If that doesn't call for a sense of humour, what does? When it came to imagining his perfect world, Utopia, the man had some amusing ideas. One was that marriages would work best if young people saw each other naked before tying the knot – something he tried out with his own daughters. When the young Sir William Roper called in search of a bride, their dad whipped off the bed sheet revealing the sisters sleeping beside each other – in the all-together. Acutely embarrassed, the outraged pair rolled on to their tummies. 'Now I have seen both sides,' chuckled their suitor, who promptly chose Margaret, the eldest, to be his wife, with whom he built a lasting marriage. QED!

UTOPIAN MARRIAGE
GUIDANCE

Now that wasn't so difficult, was it.

HAMPTON COURT

'Hampton Court?'
'No, it's just the way I move.'

Take a bow Morecambe and Wise for polishing a favourite Marxism:

Nurse: The doctor will see you now, if you'll walk this way.
Groucho: If I could do that, I wouldn't need to see the doc. *

Ah! The old ones are the best, even if they lose something to conform to the strictures of *Just A Minute*! And when it comes to Hampton Court, the venerable Tudor pile is right up there with the top royal palaces. Originally built for Cardinal Wolsey (see page 60), it was nabbed by Henry VIII who fancied a new-build by the Thames decked out with the latest mod cons: dream kitchen (covering 36,000 square feet), bathrooms to die for (the loo area that could seat 30 people) and 60 acres of gardens, with bowling greens and tennis courts. The king spent millions sprucing it up. The 15-foot tall gatehouse clock tells you the hour, the day of the month, where the Sun is relative to the Earth, the phases of the moon and its age in days, all of which helps you work out high tide on the river. Not bad for an installation timed at 1540.

---

* **R** Here again, the rules prohibit the accurate rendering of both these time-honoured exchanges – not on the grounds of decorum nor decency, but duplication (or repetition). (Alliteration has a role in marginalia too!)

CARDINAL WOLSEY

To avoid any misunderstanding, Cardinal Wolsey had no personal connection with the brand of knitwear of the same name, nor the rather upmarket range of cars that used to be seen on British roads half-a-century ago. Wolsey lived during the reign of Henry VIII, when he was second only to the king in holding sway – and, as a man of enormous girth, it took a lot of prowess, poise and devilish dexterity to keep him in position and prevent his fall. Wolsey's power and influence began to falter when his boss suffered heir loss. Having a son to follow him on the throne became a major issue for Bluff King Hal and that was soon a serious problem for Wolsey too when he failed to persuade the Pope to annul the royal marriage to childless Catherine of Aragon, so that her ex could get hitched to Anne Boleyn. That was the start of the end. Wolsey, ordered to give up his pets, surrendered the Great Seal, died in Leicester and never made it into the sarcophagus he'd commissioned for St Paul's Cathedral. Nelson's been occupying that since 1806.

THE SIXTH WIFE OF HENRY VIII

Henry VIII married six women, but depending on whether you look at it from a Catholic or an Anglican perspective, his last wife, Catherine Parr, was either his second or his fourth – not his sixth. Henry claimed that his marriage to the princess from Aragon (1st) was illegal because the Old Testament rules against a man sleeping with his brother's widow. The Pope (who didn't recognise Henry's annulments) said his second union was out, because he was still the Spanish lady's husband – that's why Henry started the Church of England. However, the king legally ended his match with Anne Boleyn (2nd) for adultery. He did the same with her namesake from Cleves (4th) because they never slept together, and with the flighty Howard girl (5th) because she went to bed with everyone, which Henry ruled as treasonable. That left Jane Seymour (3rd), his other legitimate spouse, who died while they were still a couple.*

---

* **R** Given that history records Henry VIII as having married six wives, avoiding the repetition of 'wives' and 'married' has called for quick thinking.

BLOODY MARY

Henry VIII's eldest daughter came to the throne as Mary I and tried to change the nation's drinking habits: Roman Catholic communion wines were in, Protestant beverages were out. Bloody Mary also introduced a cocktail of her own from France. This was devised in Harry's New York Bar in Paris. That was where barman Fernand Petiot mixed equal measures of tomato juice and vodka and asked a patron what he thought of it. 'Reminds me of the Bucket of Blood Club in Chicago, and a girl I knew there named Mary', was the gist of his reply. She must have been quite a dame, but not as hot as New Yorkers wanted after she and her man took up residence at the King Cole Bar at the St Regis Hotel in 1934. He spiced her up big time and Bloody Mary never looked back. The irony is that a corpse reviver for the duvet-shrouded hungover is also a grim reminder of Queen Mary's brutal inquisition that burned legions of Anglican martyrs at the stake.

COURT MUSIC

Music started to be enjoyable in the sixteenth century when period music court on. One of my ancestors was hired by Henry VIII to teach his son to play the trumpet. He was a Tudor tooter tutor. Among British monarchs the king was a very accomplished musician. He could play the flute, the harp, the keyboard and the organ. He owned hundreds of instruments, including 150 recorders – though thankfully not 'the ill woodwind that no one blows good' (aka: the oboe); that wasn't invented for another hundred years or so.* Then there's 'Greensleeves'. Tradition holds that that this was composed by Anne Boleyn's husband to please her, although another theory pinpoints it as the start of that lady's undoing:

> *King Henry vowed his wife to hurt*
> *When she sewed greensleeves on his yellow shirt.*

But, hey! You can't knock a hit. What other court music of the era has made it as the chime on ice-cream vans? Not to mention the whistled theme tune when the TV credits rolled at the close of *Lassie*?

---

* **D** You might feel that a challenge for deviation would be valid here. If the musical instrument in question (the oboe) is an anachronism (since it wasn't invented during Henry VIII's lifetime), why mention it here? But consider also that, with the constant din and droning from all the crumhorns and sackbuts played to produce court music, not having to endure Tudor oboe lessons would have been a blessed relief and therefore would not constitute a deviation.

WITCHCRAFT

If you turned your hand to witchcraft in the sixteenth century, living in Britain was a better bet than the Continent. European practitioners of black magic invariably ended up being burned or boiled alive; those sentenced to death here were hanged. But a great many Tudor exponents of witchcraft went about their business as colourful eccentrics: old dears who lived with a few pets as 'familiars', or bookish elderly men whose strange experiments were viewed as the pursuit of science, not the supernatural. Tests for witchcraft were comparatively benign in our part of the world too. Suspects were weighed against the Bible and only declared to be witches* if the good book was heavier. Down on the village pond, the guilty floated, the innocent sank (and were hauled out, if they were lucky). However, having extra bits on your body – a third nipple was very dodgy – could mark you down. It did for Anne Boleyn when she was on the slide. The beginnings of one more finger on the left hand was a sure sign that the lady was on the dark side.

* **R** Might the use of 'witchcraft' and 'witches' be grounds for a successful challenge for repetition? It's a valid point. Unlike the 'book/bookshops' debate outlined earlier, 'witchcraft' is closely associated with 'witches' since it represents the method by which (this is obviously a homophone, not a repetition!) they practise sorcery and other dark arts. You can't have 'witchcraft' without 'witches', but you could theoretically have 'bookshops' without a book – although that would place them in a perilous trading position.

WESTWARD HO!

A British navigator wasn't the first to lead an English expedition to North America. OK – Henry VII may have put up the readies, but the fellow who trousered them and commanded the voyage was a Venetian: John Cabot. Like Genoese mariner Christopher Columbus, down in the West Indies in 1492, the master of the good ship *Matthew* five years later reckoned he'd landed in Asia. Wrong again. The place where he stepped ashore was Canada. No one's sure exactly where that was, but it's a very big country. Still, he claimed the new territory for the King of England and returned triumphant, never knowing that Viking sailors had beaten him to it by five centuries. Along with the skipper, the vessel had a crew of around 20. Most came from the home port of Bristol, but there was one Dutchman (called a Burgundian in those days) and a barber from Genoa. As well as keeping hair tidy, he doubled as the doctor on board. (NB: the earlier warning about not getting ill in the Middle Ages!)

6

Elizabethan Age

THE VIRGIN QUEEN

How can anyone claiming to be Elizabeth I honestly call herself a virgin queen? But this wasn't her only royal number one. On the throne (so to speak), she was the earliest monarch to use a flushing WC. Her godson, Sir John Harrington, had designed and installed one in his own home, but sales were slow and godmother Bess ordered the second for her palace at Richmond – to keep things moving, if you catch my drift. The Virgin Queen also started a wider royal interest in personal hygiene. To the bewilderment of everyone else at court, she took a bath once a month 'whether she needed it or no'. She would certainly have approved of the 'vocal warm-up' of that wonderful Shakespearean actor, Sir Donald Sinden, who taught me the importance of diction – 'Vowels for volume, consonants for clarity' – and this … Ready now. Head up, chest out and repeat after me: Hip bath, hip … er … er …*

---

* **R** Disaster! Catastrophe! I have to self-challenge. The exercise works a treat, but the rules don't allow its recitation because it's riddled with repetition – as you can tell. And that made me hesitate. I thought I was serving an ace and ended with a double-fault! Readers might be interested to know what they missed in this rendition. Sir Donald Sinden's memorable vocal exercise comprised repeating three times the line: Hip bath, hip bath, lavatory, lavatory, bidet, bidet, douche!

SIR FRANCIS DRAKE

How about a clerihew* to start beating Drake's drum?

> *Playing bowls, Sir Francis Drake*
> *On Plymouth Hoe did ages take*
> *For the game proved so much harder*
> *Than beating the Armada.*

He 'singed the King of Spain's beard at Cadiz', bowled out the opposition fleet near the Devon port and organised the first British round-the-world cruise, or as the schoolboy howler puts it: 'Sir Francis Drake circumcised the world in a 100-foot clipper which was very dangerous to all his men.' Now, there's something to make you sit up and think, or wince – depending on your point of view. Mind you, if you were a naughty Spanish child, running your mother ragged even as late as the twentieth century she was still likely to utter the dire threat, 'El Draque will get you' – and this was 400 years after he attacked and terrorised their shipping. No wonder they feel prickly about Gibraltar. Drake's raid in 1587 destroyed over 30 vessels getting ready for an invasion of Britain, which set back Philip II's plan by a year.

I thought singeing my beard was a figure of speech!

---

* It would be unfair not to explain the clerihew to the unaware, though perhaps not directly under the heading 'Francis Drake'. As tersely as possible, then:

> *Edmund Clerihew Bentley*
> *Devised a verse form that mocks, albeit gently*
> *AABB's the rhyme*
> *And lines two and four can go on for really quite some protracted time.*

THE ROYAL NAVY

Winston Churchill famously summed up the Royal Navy in three words: rum, sodomy and the lash – or five, if you prefer 'bum' and 'baccy' to follow the initial word. It probably wasn't that different in the sixteenth century, but Elizabeth I, who had a soft spot for man's best friend, let her Sea Dogs run loose on the Spanish Main, and gave them vessels with which they scoffed their fill. When Philip II decided that was too much, he unleashed his own Spaniels to hunt down Sir Francis Drake – who had a price of several million pounds on his head – and to invade England to punish the queen for being such a bitch to the Papal Sealyham after she had been excommunicated for misbehaving in the Roman Catholic Church. But the English seaside weather in July 1588 was vile. So, the king's crews went to the Low Countries instead. They weren't any better – nor were Scotland and Ireland. But by then Gloriana was celebrating an epic victory and had started to enjoy life in a Golden Cage.

MARY QUEEN OF SCOTS

You know the nursery rhyme:

> *Mary, Mary quite contrary*
> *How does your garden grow,*
> *With silver bells and cockle shells*
> *And pretty maids all in a row.*

But are you aware of the fact that one reading of it is direct reference to the tragic life of Good Queen Bess's fetching cousin, Mary Queen of Scots? According to this line of thought, the argentine chimes and small marine casings were ornaments that decorated a dress given to Mary by her first husband, the Dauphin of France. And the fair maidens lined up at the end of the verse? They were her ladies-in-waiting, the famous Four Marys: Mary Seton, Mary Fleming, Mary Beaton and Mary Livingston. Mary (the queen) seems to have suffered from astonishing bad luck on the long-term health front. Aside from losing her head to her cousin, her young spouse died a year into their marriage and her second was murdered. Mary herself was afflicted by depression, hysteria, smallpox, liver disease, convulsions, chlorosis, gastric ulcers, porphyria, measles, nervous collapses, rheumatism, vomiting and, near the end of her days, permanent lameness.*

* **R** Clever slaloming through the rules of *Just A Minute*. The unwary player might inadvertently have repeated the 'silver bells and cockle shells' of the rhyme, while overlooking the totally valid repetition of the name Mary no fewer than ten times. Well played!

JOUSTING

How long does a jousting tournament last? Until knightfall! What do you call a knight who jousts all the time? Sir Lancelot! What's the 60-second warm-up for a joust known as? A game of 'Joust a Minute' – natch. Enough of this punning persiflage. Let's get down to business. Jousting is a martial sport – known in the Middle Ages as a hastilude – in which two heroic horse-riders wielding lances with blunted tips challenge one another, often as part of a tournament. The contest is traditionally between worthy adversaries who enter the lists and strive to unseat their opponents without taking a tumble themselves. In the second half of the sixteenth century the high point of the Elizabethan jousting calendar was the Accession Day tilts, held annually on 17 November, to mark Queen Elizabeth's coronation. Competitors spent eye-watering sums to kit out themselves and their retainers in all manner of outlandish fancy dress. Poets joined in the fun writing impenetrable allegorical verses (see page 74) and drafting obsequious speeches for their patrons. Good Queen Bess loved every bit of it.

SIR WALTER RALEIGH

Sir Walter Raleigh had it made. He was blessed with matinée-idol good looks, had a way with the ladies and the queen was hot for him. No wonder posterity has given him a good run. All right, he made a name for himself in the bicycle business, but so did Noddy. It's what Sir Walter didn't do that narks we lesser mortals. He's celebrated for laying his magnificent cloak over a puddle so that Gloriana wouldn't get her dainty shoes wet. Our man gets the credit for introducing tobacco from the New World. History also reports that he brought us the potato. But I refer you to Henry Ford on historiography, quoted earlier. Sir Walter Raleigh did none of these. That whatsit with the cape thingy? It's a bit of whimsy spun by Thomas Fuller and embroidered by Sir Walter Scott. The dreaded weed? Francis Drake gave Raleigh his first drag, after Sir John Hawkins had brought it to England. Spuds? Frankie D again, after he'd imported a load from Italy.

What ARE you?!

A potato.

BOIL ME and MASH me up!

THE FAERIE QUEENE

He wouldn't be allowed to publish it today, not with that title. But Edmund Spenser was writing in more innocent times. Or was he? This poem is shot through with allegory; Elizabethan word-smiths were very big on the verse form. Remember 'Mary quite contrary'? It's charming, unless you interpret the 'silver bells' as thumbscrews, 'cockle shells' as other implements of torture, and 'pretty maids all in a row' as victims of religious persecution. That's why cleverly disguising the meaning of what you wrote wasn't a bad idea. Anyhow, the sovereign ordered her treasurer to pay £100 for *The Fairie Queene* (she does take centre stage after all). William Cecil told her that was excessive. 'Then give him what is reason,' she replied. But he still didn't pay up. Time passed and when they next met, the poet gave his monarch this quatrain of delicate complaint:

> *I was promis'd on a time,*
> *To have a reason for my rhyme:*
> *From that moment unto this season,*
> *I receiv'd neither of the aforementioned.* *

I know it doesn't scan, but the rules on repetition must be observed and you catch the drift. Anyhow, it did the trick and the man with the money had to cough up the original hundred quid!

---

* ℝ In case you may not have guessed it, the word replaced by the necessary inclusion of 'aforementioned' (to dodge repetition) is 'reason'.

MERRIE ENGLAND

Merrie England opened at London's Savoy Theatre on the second day of the fourth month of 1902 (thereby avoiding the April Fool's Day banana skin with the critics that could have brought about its immediate closure) and ran for 120 performances before going on tour and becoming a mainstay of amateur operatic companies – with characters like Jill-All-Alone, Silas Simpkins, Long Tom and Big Ben what part-time thespian would turn down a role? This gem of a comic opera conjures up a bygone age, so far distant because the kind of jolly arcadian England it evokes never really existed, let alone in the sixteenth century. All the same, when the New Elizabethan Age dawned, the coronation year witnessed over 500 non-professional productions and at Luton Hoo they went completely over the top, making it a colossal pageant with a cast of nearly 1000. The plot, which would have done justice to the pen of the Bard, is centred on love rivalries at court where a billet-doux written by Sir Walter Raleigh to one of the royal ladies-in-waiting ends up in the hands of the queen herself. Whoops!

GUY FAWKES

History remembers Guy Fawkes as the earliest proponent of the Big Bang Theory and a pioneer of rockets. But the dark arts of Westminster subterfuge nearly blew up in his face. Basically, this Guy was an old-fashioned fellow. Change wasn't his style. He liked things the way they used to be and that meant turning the clock back at least a century with a Roman Catholic realm and a native-born monarch on the throne. His problem in 1605* was that the country didn't have either. The crown was currently being sported by a king who swung both ways: he couldn't decide whether he was James I of England or James VI of Scotland, so went for the two together. Fawkes's other dilemma was that he was a fall-Guy. Who in their right mind would get caught with 36 barrels of gunpowder and a lighter in the cellars of the House of Lords the night before the State Opening of Parliament? Still, he was a martyr to the cause and ever since children have been collecting funds in his memory.

* If only there were some *Just A Minute*-compliant rhyme for remembering a more precise date.

THE MAYFLOWER

The *Mayflower* was an English ship commissioned in the reign of Elizabeth I, but built in the time of her successor, King James, and made famous because of the transatlantic crossing the vessel took 17 years after her demise in the year one thousand six hundred and three. Yes, in the fall of 1620, as Indigenous Americans living on the coast of Massachusetts were turning their thoughts to Thanksgiving and Black Friday sales, different kinds of sails blew in over the horizon. The *Mayflower* brought travellers – well-intentioned pilgrims – from the Old World to the New. They were six months later than they should have been. They planned to plant crops, but the ground soon froze. They hungrily watched fish but had no tackle with which to catch any. Snow fell knee-deep, but they had left their snowshoes at home too. The *Mayflower* was their refuge for that first winter and disease killed off half the party. So much for the American dream, which would have turned nightmare if locals hadn't brought them food. Come the spring, they went ashore and started in the real estate business. 'We verily believe and trust the Lord is with us, and that he will graciously prosper our endeavours', they declared. Judging by the price of shore-line properties in the Cape Cod area today, He did. Kerching!

WASHING TIMELINE on which
history has been hung out
to dry any old how...

7

Shakespeare & Co

WILLIAM SHAKESPEARE

Reckoned second only to Wayne Rooney as the finest exponent of the English language, William Shakespeare was born in Stratford, centuries before it hosted the Olympic Games. Internationally acclaimed, it is a wonder that he came to be accepted in his home country after his agent's unfortunate turn of phrase in promoting his client as 'Bard from England'. Some scholars believe that Shakespeare's works were written by his chum Francis Bacon, but what self-respecting actor would want to join the Royal Bacon Company?* Although he married Anne Hathaway, he was not tempted to emigrate and live with her in New York. He wrote lots of poetry and at least 37 plays, often taking the stories from other people's works. His *Romeo and Juliet*, for example, is based on *West Side Story*. Or is it the other way around? No, it can't be – I've never heard of a play called *Juliet and Romeo*.† William Shakespeare famously died on his birthday. It's incredible the amount he achieved in those few hours.

Waaaaaaaaa...

* **R** There is repetition of Bacon, but a sympathetic reader would give the benefit of the doubt because it's not a bad joke even if it's a very old one.

† **R** Repetition of Juliet and Romeo right at the end demonstrates that even skilled wordsmiths can let down their guard. A successful challenger has only to deliver a couple of challenge-free sentences to win the round and claim the point, where the wording 'with that title' instead of the repeated phrase, would have secured it for the writer.

THE UPSTART CROW

Shakespeare was nicknamed the Upstart Crow, as Ben Elton will cheerfully tell you. Why? Because the Bard of Avon was a boy from the Midlands. Local uni (Warwick) lay 400 years off and, despite bashing away at English, young Will wasn't an Oxbridge man – unlike published peers Kit Marlowe (Benet [now Corpus Christi], Cambridge), Sir Walter Raleigh (Oriel, Oxon) and Robert Greene (Clare, Cantab for BA/St John's for MA – maybe the other place too). But the Stratford boy sidestepped this setback, polished his penmanship as a jobbing actor and took flight. That stuck in the craw of RG, who did his own plays no favours with titles like *The Scottish Historie of James the fourth, slaine at Flodden*. While his *Groatsworth of Wit* is only saved by the celebrated dig at the 'upstart crow, beautified with our feathers, that, with his Tygers heart wrapt in a Players hide, supposes he is as well able to bumbast out a blanke verse as the best of you.' But the Crow had the last laugh on television with the actor cast to play him: David Mitchell was educated at Peterhouse, in the university beside the River Cam.*

---

* **R** A number of alternative names for our two oldest universities enable you to identify various seats of learning within them without laying the rendition open to challenge for repetition. The writer does come close to hesitation on a couple of occasions where the subject changes, but manages to keep going. And keep going he does, as you may have spotted.

SHAKESPEARE'S GLOBE

Judging by his shaky grasp of geography, Shakespeare's Globe couldn't have been up to much. If he did indeed spend time in Italy, it's odd how little notice he took of his surroundings. Valentine, one of his *Two Gentlemen of Verona*, describes sailing from there cross-country to Milan – duh! In *The Winter's Tale* he gives land-locked Bohemia a coastline. Hamlet's chums, Rosencrantz and Guildenstern, do at least take ship for England, they just complete the North Sea passage in half the time it would have taken an Elizabethan vessel. Back in Denmark, Elsinore is given cliffs (there aren't any). In fairness, all the world was a stage in Shakespeare's day – with serious limitations. Take the Prologue in *Henry V*:

> *... can this cockpit hold*
> *The vasty field of France? Or may we cram*
> *Within this wooden O the very casques*
> *That did affright the air at Agincourt?*

Evidently drawn to the Alps, his vocabulary is the first to record 'luggage', 'mountaineer' and 'summit'. However, another 'new' word sums up his understanding of global topography: 'Laughable'.

SHAKESPEARE'S GLOBE

It's blank!

UNKNOWN
UNIMAGINED
NEVER VISITED
UNDISCOVERED
UNEXPLORED

HAMLET

Having essayed the role myself, I think there's a good deal I can tell you about Hamlet, assuming you mean the character in the Shakespeare play rather than the small cheroot of the same name. My favourite theatrical Hamlets include Benedict Cumberbatch, Freddie Fox, Eddie Izzard (a solo Hamlet and sensational), Maxine Peake (a fine female Hamlet, following in the footsteps of the legendary Sarah Bernhardt), Sir Ian McKellen (at 82 the oldest Hamlet ever), and myself. When I first played Hamlet I was very young and the critics didn't like it. The reviews were all stinkers. The audience didn't think much of my performance either. In fact, they threw eggs at me. Yes, I went on as Hamlet and came off as omelette. And I'd tried so hard to understand the part. I remember talking to one of the old actors in the company – he'd been a Hamlet years before, but he was now giving us his Polonius. Anyway, I wanted to know about the relationship between Hamlet and the fair Ophelia – how intimate were they? 'Do you think Hamlet sleeps with her?' I asked him. He said, 'I don't know about the West End, laddie, but we always did on tour.'

ROMEO AND JULIET

Romeo and Juliet is a tragedy famed for its romantic verse:

> *'Twas in a restaurant they met,*
> *Romeo and Juliet –*
> *He had no money to pay the debt,*
> *So Romee owed what Julie ate!*

But the play raises serious relationship issues for present-day audiences. Romeo is on the rebound after Rosaline when he pitches up at the Capulet party. His judgement is impaired and then he catches sight of his ex's cousin. What's his driver? Revenge? Point scoring? Chick scoring? Take your pick. Neither Romeo nor Juliet lose any time before hurling themselves into the disastrous love-in that ends up killing a shedload of the cast. What's with the Bard? Deadline pressure to get the job finished? They're off on their first date before you can say 'A plague on both your houses'. Next comes the whirlwind marriage, followed by the reception brawl that finishes off Mercutio and Tybalt – and then it's 'Cheerio, Romeo'. Maybe the playwright forestalled bad reviews with the closing lines:

> *For never was a story of more woe*
> *Than this of Juliet and her Romeo.*

ROMEO ON THE REBOUND

MACBETH

For never was a story of more strife
Than that of Macbeth and his scary wife.

The Bard piles on further twenty-first-century angst in his Scottish play. Energy crises, environmental meltdown, fake news, knife crime – *Macbeth* has it all. Forget any charm offensive too. Shakespeare uses reverse psychology from curtain-up and the dystopian existence of three weird sisters in reduced circumstances. Through them we learn: one-pot cookery without fossil fuels; to eschew red meat for unfamiliar sources of protein; how to cope with toxic pollution; and to be wary of self-serving wannabes on the make. Enter the Macbeths, a power-hungry couple who'd kill for the main prize. And here our boy Bill plays an ace: they get it and then lose the lot. She can't sleep and goes doolally because the washing-machine dies and dealing with laundry becomes a nightmare. Limited to dwindling candlelight, he sees daggers and ghosts at every turn. Worst of all, their life becomes 'a tale told by an idiot'. Could this be false modesty by a playwright with an eye on a BAFTA?

KING LEAR

King Lear, Shakespeare's analysis of dysfunctional family life and the deep schisms caused by poor inheritance planning, is right up there with today's misery memoirs. Duped by two scheming female offspring, the dotty old king descends into senile ramblings, evinced by snatches of the verse form that he'd picked up in Ireland, such as:

> *The fortunes of families they fall and they rise,*
> *A king driven mad plus a dad with no eyes.*
> *So last shall be first,*
> *The best gets the worst.*
> *Now who is the foolish and which one's the wise?*

Or this:

> *The ancient and tragic King Lear*
> *Went out on the heath full of fear.*
> *Instead of his howling,*
> *And whining and yowling,*
> *He should have gone out for a beer.**

That's the kind of straight-talking, no-nonsense, directing every dramatist craves. All actors too. Peter Ustinov, cast to play Lear in the 1979 production at Stratford, Ontario, remarked testily before opening, 'I've got three daughters, which is a more thorough rehearsal for the part than anything ['method'-acting guru] Stanislavski ever suggested.'

---

* A serendipitous juxtaposition of topic and available material results in an engaging union that is both informative and entertaining. In this case linking King Lear with the master of the limerick produces some unexpected insights into Shakespeare's work.

A MIDSUMMER NIGHT'S DREAM

A Midsummer Night's Dream does tend to bring out what one might term 'the inventive' in directors. Some of their ideas work well. Shortly before my own spell among Oxford's dreaming spires, Nevill Coghill had a pontoon submerged in the gardens of Worcester College so that Puck seemed to be gliding over the surface – brilliant. On the other hand, back in 1933, the celebrated Max Reinhardt was booked to direct the same play in the city. This was to be his last production in England and caused quite a stir, especially when he demanded 'eighty extras and a lake'. Then, surveying his chosen site for the first time, he pointed to the distant rooftops of Headington, and commented airily, 'that village over there must be removed'. The Bard would be thrilled by his daring. After all, his plot calls for a fairy to fall in love with Bottom temporarily disguised as an ass, because she won't hand over her page boy to her husband. If that doesn't get the psycho-analysts working overtime, I don't know what will.

I must be asleep and this is only a dream.

THE COMEDY OF ERRORS

Shakespeare's subconscious must have been giving him a hard time when he called this wacky early play *The Comedy of Errors*. Fair dos, the plot lines are ludicrous (even by the standards of Elizabethan knockabout stage humour): when two sets of identical twins, accidentally separated at birth, are given freedom to spread madcap mayhem and confusion from curtain-up to the final bow. But what private demons was the Bard trying to exorcise here? Not for the first time he'd nicked the idea from someone else; in this case, Roman playwright, Plautus. Did it hint at deep-rooted anxieties about shortcomings in his own classical education? He has a clock striking the hour in *Julius Caesar*, a millennium before the timepiece was invented. Careless! Still in the ancient world, this alumnus of Stratford grammar school rolls billiards into *Antony and Cleopatra* at least 15 centuries too early! For a real turkey, though, look to his *Henry IV* plays where the eponymous bird* is mentioned 250 years before the first strutted ashore in England in the mid-sixteenth century.

---

* **R** Nice avoidance of repetition: 'eponymous' is a valuable adjective and here it is deployed very effectively.

SHAKESPEARE'S GREAT CONTEMPORARIES

Several of Shakespeare's contemporaries were truly great dramatists and it's a tragedy that their work is too often overlooked. Christopher Marlowe had a stab at long-term fame by using at least seven versions of his surname and dying in mysterious circumstances. Ben Jonson gets the odd revival here and there. But how often these days do you see people queuing for a double bill of John Dekker, re-tuning an old Ford, or searching for a lost Kyd? Could it be that their run-ins with the authorities have done them no favours? I know that Shakespeare may have made a swift exit from Stratford after being fingered for poaching, but he became a wealthy and respected member of society. Whereas the author of *Every Man in His Humour* was arrested for killing another playwright and was thumb-branded as punishment. The writer of *The Shoemaker's Holiday* spent time in a debtor's prison. While the one sharing his name with a riverside town in Buckinghamshire always lived on the edge, doubling as a secret agent and mingling with plotters against the queen before being knifed down the Thames in Deptford.*

* A knowledge of both Shakespeare's contemporary playwrights and their work facilitates this playful account of their lives and times. There's a satisfying balance, with references to Christopher Marlowe bookending the entry, while the names of three of Shakespeare's contemporaries lend themselves to pleasing wordplay.

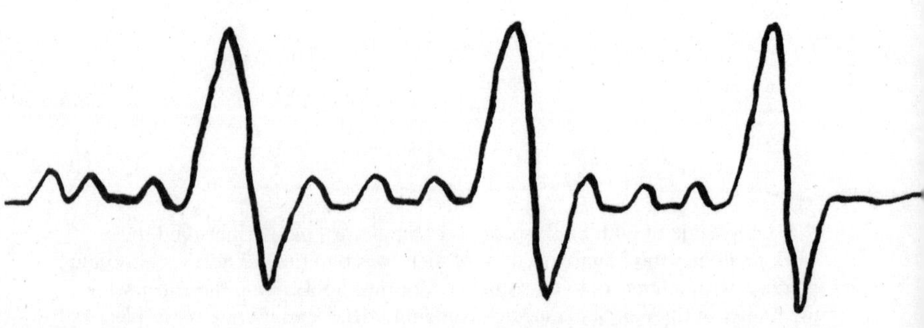

8

Proper Charlies

CHARLES I

Charles I committed the classic error of letting top-billing go to his head, which he maintained until he lost it on some scaffolding in Whitehall. His mistake was in believing that God had made him sovereign ruler and therefore given him a free hand to govern as he wished – never a sound policy. But then, Charles I was a short-arse, barely 5 feet 4 inches high. The king tried to get round this by commissioning artists to depict him as taller. The sculptor Hubert Le Sueur, called on to show Charles on horseback, was told to make his steed 'bigger than a greate Horsse by a foot', and its royal rider 'proportionable full six feet'. The fact that we can see his work to this day in Charing Cross is down to a wily scrap-metal dealer from Holborn, who was told to melt it down during the Commonwealth (see page 94). Hedging his bets, he buried the statue intact, sold off brass-handled cutlery he claimed was made from the bronze, and then dug it up when the monarchy was restored.

Without my head
I'm even shorter.

ROUNDHEADS AND CAVALIERS

The esteemed authors of *1066 and All That* tell us all we need to know about these opposing factions in the civil wars that raged in Britain in the seventeenth century. On one side stood the Cavaliers, loyal to the absolute power of the king, staunch defenders of the established order of lace collars, flowing locks and large, over-the-top, feather-adorned hats, who were characterised by Sellar and Yeatman as 'Wrong but Wromantic'. Opposing them were the Roundheads, the pro-Parliamentary grouping who were OK with having a monarch on the throne – providing it was one that the people's elected representatives (i.e. Roundheads themselves) could control. Decked out in sober outfits, sensible short haircuts and leather jerkins, they are described as 'Right but Repulsive'. The legacy of their conflict survives in unexpected places. Take the nursery rhyme 'Humpty Dumpty sat on a wall'.* According to some sources, this is an account of the downfall of a whopping great Cavalier cannon, mounted on a church in Colchester during the fighting in Essex.

---

* **D** A cunning diversionary tactic like this can throw the concentration of readers, struggling to keep up after the announcement of the nursery rhyme. This buys the author valuable seconds as the whistle blast beckons.

OLIVER CROMWELL – WARTS AND ALL

Oliver Cromwell may have threatened that he wouldn't pay the painter Sir Peter Lely a farthing for his portrait unless he did 'but remark all these roughnesses, pimples, warts and everything as you see me', but when it came to personal make-up he had different advice for his followers. With a name like the New Model Army,* personal appearance was top priority – for them and their style guru. 'Put your trust in God,' Cromwell told the adoring throng as they were about to make another entrance, before warning everyone to look after their compacts, 'but mind you keep your powder dry.' The Lord Protector of England, and head of the Commonwealth that replaced the monarchy after Charles I lost his head, was a master of power networking. Legend holds that on the eve of the Battle of Worcester, he cut a seven-year deal with the Devil in return for victory. Cromwell won the battle, but 84 months later, to the day, he died on 3 September 1658.

---

* Oliver Cromwell would turn in his grave, but redirecting the name for his military force creates the happy opportunity for gentle fun at his expense.

SUE PERKINS ON ...
THE PURITANS

The Puritan period lasted from 1620 to 1750, though it felt much longer than that. It's safe to say, the Puritans were the least fun of all the English Protestant splinter groups. Their leader, Oliver Cromwell, banned Christmas, which created a black market for mince pies. The populous carried on celebrating the festival in private, pushing it underground and inspiring the first Secret Santa. The Puritans felt that the date of Jesus's birthday was simply about getting smashed and over-indulging. And they were right. But it's also about avoiding your grandma when she goes into a war anecdote. The Puritans extended their sourness to public art, banning theatres and dancing. This meant *The Mousetrap* was forced to close for a couple of years, though people were good enough to keep the ending schtum. To focus the mind on higher pursuits, the Puritans declared one day in every month should be reserved for fasting; thereby initiating the 30–1 diet. Puritans hated music, both choral and instrumental, and liked nothing more than smashing up ecclesiastical organs. The poor pipes of Worcester Cathedral took a hell of a beating during the Civil War, courtesy of an axe. Coincidentally, this was the worst severing of an organ until Lorena Bobbitt came along in 1993.

Lovely to have a few christmases off.

OLD ROWLEY

Old Rowley was a stallion with a reputation for siring fine foals and, with his roving eye and reputation for enjoying spirited mounts, Charles II was a shoo-in for the nickname. Equine quadrupeds were significant features of his reign – and before it. After escaping defeat at the Battle of Worcester, the would-be king made his somewhat ponderous flight to the Continent astride a mill horse. Eager to get away and used to sprightlier rides, the royal fugitive began to complain about his steed's pace – or lack of it. 'No wonder, sire, that the nag goes heavily,' replied the miller, huffily defending his trusty nag, 'as it bears the weight of three kingdoms on its back.' Touché! In happier times, and now on the throne, the Merry Monarch regularly attended race meetings at Newmarket. Around 1665 he inaugurated the Town Plate and six years later became the first (and to date the only) reigning sovereign to gallop home a winner.

NELL GWYN

After starting out in the greengrocery business, Nell Gwyn entered the earliest rounds of *Britain's Got Talent* and launched a career among the first actresses on the English stage. As the self-styled 'Protestant whore', she was popular with the general public and even more so with King Charles II, who was a huge admirer of her theatre work and an even greater devotee of what she got up to behind the scenes. Historians record over a dozen royal mistresses who enjoyed the Merry Monarch's favours, and there are likely to have been many other casual or secret acquaintances, but 'witty, pretty Nell' remained a favourite throughout his life. She bore him a son and one day was overheard by the king shouting, 'Come here, you little bastard.' When the boy's father ticked her off for using such coarse language, she replied, 'But, sire, I have no better name to call him by.' Her royal lover took the hint, and the lad soon bore the titles Baron of Headington and Earl of Burford.

SAMUEL PEPYS

Samuel Pepys was a big cheese in Charles II's navy and it's thanks to his diary that we know Pepys's interest in dairy* produce wasn't restricted to his day job. When his home was threatened by the Great Fire of London (see page 100), he buried his most valuable possessions in the garden: savings in gold, important documents and – pride of his larder – a huge wheel of Parmesan. His tastes ranged far and wide. The journal records him as the first person in England to drink a cup of tea. He had a keen eye for the ladies and recorded numerous affairs with servants, the wives, daughters and occasionally mothers of colleagues. As a special natal-anni-versary-treat-to-self in 1669, he took himself, Mrs Pepys and their household to Westminster Abbey. There they found the open coffin and the 232-year-old corpse of Henry V's consort on which, Pepys noted: 'I did kiss her mouth, reflecting upon it that I did kiss a Queen, and that this was my birth-day, 36 years old.'

* Note the orthographical byplay. The words 'diary' and 'dairy' look almost identical because they are spelled with the same letters, and at a quick glance could be mistaken visually as a repetition. However, aurally they are clearly different.

KEEPING A DIARY

I must declare an interest – well, a couple to be honest.* I am both a lifelong fan of Oscar Wilde and a recorder of my own life. So, when Gwendolen tells Cecily in *The Importance of Being Earnest*, 'I never travel without my diary. One should have something sensational to read in the train,' who am I to quibble (particularly when her words serve as a handy title)?† Two of the foremost exponents of personal reportage in the English language, Samuel Pepys and John Evelyn, set down their lives in the seventeenth century. Sam's work covers approaching a decade, a small fraction of the 91-year-long account of Col. Ernest Loftus of Harare, Zimbabwe, who made his final entry aged 178 days after his 103rd birthday. Mind you, it could be argued that the Carolean chronicler used his native language sparingly, opting at times for shorthand and a code employing French, Spanish and Italian words, especially for the fruitier bits. Johnny E, however, started his life's coverage as a student aged 20 in 1640 and maintained it until he died aged 86.‡

---

* Risky move so close to the beginning. This tactic calls for careful handling and swift execution if it's not to be pounced on for hesitation.

† *Something Sensational to Read in the Train: The Diary of a Lifetime* by Gyles Brandreth, published some years ago and still available in some branches of Oxfam.

‡ **R** Writing about two of the greatest diarists in the English language without repeating 'diarists' or 'language' isn't easy. It is successfully negotiated in this example through some canny circumlocution.

THE GREAT FIRE OF LONDON

The Great Fire of London ignited in 1666 when fake news was all the rage. England was at war with Holland (and France, which had joined in for good measure). Anti-monarchy, Papist plots were suspected everywhere. Puritan distaste for excess was shoving its oar in to condemn 'gluttony' and greed in London's commercial heartland. Then disaster struck. The city blazed uncontrollably for five days and all of the above were blamed for starting the devastating conflagration. Only later, while they were still damping down the ashes, did it become clear that the cause of the Great Fire of London had been a spark from a baker's oven in Pudding Lane – you couldn't make it up. Even better, the fire eventually petered out at Pye Corner. But it left in smouldering ruins the homes of well over 70,000 Londoners, St Paul's Cathedral and all but 22 of the 109 parish churches, as well as most of capital's administrative buildings. But alternative facts continued to proliferate, among them an official death toll of less than ten. Really?

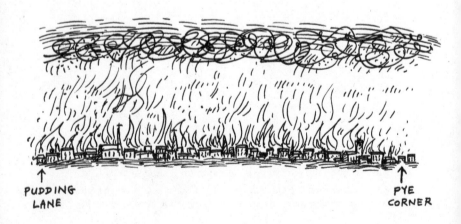

PUDDING
LANE

PYE
CORNER

SIR CHRISTOPHER WREN

Sir Christopher Wren is rightly hailed as Britain's greatest architect, remembered in timeless verse like this:

> Sir Christopher Wren
> Said, 'I am going to dine with some men.
> If anyone calls
> Say I am designing St Paul's.'

It's just tough that this London landmark has eclipsed his genius in other spheres. Appointed Professor of Astronomy at Oxford before he was 30, you can see that Wren had more than a smattering of self-confidence. There's further evidence in Windsor's Guildhall. The story goes that Wren was involved in its design. However, local building inspectors weren't convinced by his calculations. Doubts were raised about the stone pillars. The men from the town planning department questioned whether Wren had specified enough supports to hold up the structure above. He didn't agree with his detractors, kept schtum and added four more. Only these don't actually reach all the way to the ceiling: there's a small, virtually imperceptible gap where each one stops short – so difficult to see that the inspectors signed off the work and it still stands.

SIR ISAAC NEWTON

It's thanks to Newton that we know about gravity; are able to perform advanced mathematical calculations (all right, others can); understand the laws of motion; and have reflecting telescopes. Lesser known was his contribution to workplace health and safety from more recent times as demonstrated in this mantra from the construction industry:

Sir Isaac Newton told us why every apple drops from the sky,
And from this fact, it's very plain, other objects do the same.
A brick, a bolt, a bar, a cup, invariably falls down, not up –
And every common device and tool is governed by this very rule.
So when you handle them up there, let your watchword be, 'Take Care'.
If on high, you drop a spanner, it travels in a downward manner.
At work, a fifth of accidents or more, illustrate old Newton's law.
But one thing he forgot to add, the damage won't be half as bad
If you are wearing proper clothes, especially on your head and toes.
These hats and shoes are there to save their user from an early grave. *

---

* **D** A well-judged example of how a passage of verse, or similar recitation, can occupy a substantial portion of a minute-long delivery. The example above succeeds in avoiding challenges for deviation by repeating the name Newton and by its focus on his work on gravity.

9

By George!

THE UNION OF ENGLAND AND SCOTLAND

It took over a century for Scotland and England to start making a go of it together, which rather sums up their on–off relationship ever since. It began when Queen Elizabeth I died, hairless,* in 1603 and the son of Mary Queen of Scots pitched up as King James I. That fused the two crowns. Uniting the parliaments wasn't as straightforward, but by the start of the seventeen hundreds they were formally conjoined and remained so for almost all the next three. The Acts of Union came into effect in seventeen hundred and seven, but references to them still arouse personal sensitivities. Wind forward to 1994 and yours truly is an MP, steering an innocent private member's bill through parliament so that people could marry in licensed places that weren't either churches or register offices. I'm pleased to say that it succeeded and became law. Less happy during its passage were the frequent, although perfectly understandable, references to me as 'an expert on the marriage act' – remarks that made my wife laugh so much she nearly fell out of her bunk!†

* Pleasing *paronomasia* (a pun) linking two of Good Queen Bess's major disappointments: baldness in old age and the lack of a Tudor successor.

† Further verbal verisimilitude occasioned by the word 'union'.

OUR FIRST PRIME MINISTER

British politics is wonderful in its absurdities – and I should know. Here's Sir Robert Walpole, the first senior political occupant of 10 Downing Street, and I suppose next door at number 11 too, since he had both jobs: First Lord of the Treasury and Chancellor of the Exchequer. He's come down through history as our first prime minister, although he never called himself that, and he held on to the post for longer than any of his successors principally because, without him, government in this country would have pretty much fallen apart. The national problem, and Bob's ticket to power, lay in the palace occupied by the German-speaking Hanoverian dynasty. First up was King George I, of whom the deliciously waspish Lady Mary Wortley Montagu once observed, 'In private life he would have been called an honest blockhead.' He carried that tray into politics by quickly ceasing to preside over his 'Council-board' because he couldn't understand English; instead, leaving Bobby to take charge of a 'Cabinet' of Ministers. When his son became sovereign, he was scarcely better equipped linguistically than his dad, so Bobsie stuck around to carry on his 'good' work – for almost 21 years in total.

ROYAL ASCOT

Ascot has royal associations that date back to the reign of the last Stuart sovereign. Barely a brisk canter down the road from Windsor Castle, the Berkshire town's open heath was conveniently located for the pursuit of her equestrian interests, and ever since its inauguration in 1711 the annual race meeting has traditionally opened with a barbecue in her honour: the Queen Anne Steaks. Horse-racing* became popularly referred to as the 'sport of kings', but women members of Britain's royal house have challenged that emphatically. Royal Ascot's founder's namesake[†] is known world-wide today as a champion competitor who once took part as a jockey at Ascot herself. In addition, the Princess Royal has been acclaimed as the nation's games' personality of the year, as well as a winner of three top European medals for riding, and she was the first royal to participate in the television quiz show about similar physical recreations, not to mention the Olympics. Her mother, our present Queen, triumphed at Royal Ascot herself in 2013, when her filly Estimate won the Gold Cup – the only time it has ever gone to a reigning monarch.

---

* The worlds of horse-racing commentary and *Just A Minute* tend to keep themselves separate, to the relief of anyone trying to imagine going up against, say, The Sage of Halifax, Jim McGrath, whose fluency would quash any chance of a challenge. FACT: the British Council recommends learners of English study commentary on the nags.

† ℝ Smart avoidance of the repetition of the name 'Anne', coupled with a serendipitous melding of the Stuart monarch and our present monarch's daughter.

FARMER GEORGE

Farmer George, or His Majesty King George III, as he probably preferred to be known, was truly a man of his time. Eighteenth-century publishers with an eye on the main chance were piling into the booming agricultural sector, where works like *The Farmer's Letters to the People of England, Rural Oeconomy* and *The improved culture of three principal grasses, lucerne, sainfoin, and burnet* were flying off the shelves. Heading the pack was *Horse-hoeing Husbandry* by rock star turned agronomist Jethro Tull. For once, growing food was as cool as cooking it and George III rolled up his sleeves and jumped on the hay cart. (Being called George was a help: it's a pun on the Greek word '*geōrgos*' (γεωργός), meaning 'a farmer'.) But Georgie's interests ranged beyond the agrarian. In 1760 he commissioned a state-of-the-art gold coach that his successors have been travelling about in ever since. A year later he bought them a comfy London home called Buckingham House. Farmer George also gave the book trade a boost by donating 65,000 of his volumes to start a national library. It seems a shame that he went bonkers and ended his days talking to trees.

BONNIE PRINCE CHARLIE

When you find yourself christened Charles Edward Louis John Casimir Sylvester Severino Maria Stuart, it's understandable that any name is going to sound better, even the mildly ambiguous Bonnie Prince Charlie. As the would-be monarch of Scotland, England and Ireland, Bonnie Prince Charlie spent just 14 months in Britain during the rebellion he led from 1745, plus a very brief return, incognito, four years later. He saw out the rest of his days on the Continent, bitter and peevish that his claim to the British throne was ended on a bleak Scottish moorland. For a frankly inept rebel leader, this grandson of exiled James II was far more successful with devotees of Och-aye-hoots-and-away-mon folk-song* than he ever was leading unruly clansmen against well-drilled redcoats. It's understandable if he played down lyrics which emphasise his hasty exit after the defeat at Culloden, although Robert Louis Stevenson does offer modest cheer with this warming cocktail of his own creation:

> Mull was astern, Rum on the port,
> Eigg off the starboard bow;†
> Glory of youth glowed in his soul;
> Where is that grandeur now?

---

* Outdated stereotypical turns of phrase like this are rightly frowned upon these days, but repetition of the word 'Scottish' had to be avoided somehow.

† **D** Deviation: The rhythm will sound familiar to anyone who knows the 'Skye Boat Song' ('Speed bonnie boat ...'), a Jacobite air which Stevenson thought in need of improvement, prompting him to write the new lyrics which remain less popular to this day.

THE ENGLISH GARDEN

Don't believe anyone who tells you the English garden has nothing to do with politics. Just look at the Wars of the Roses (see page 52). They began with a gardening tiff. Where did David Cameron and Nick Clegg launch their coalition government in 2010? The garden of 10 Downing Street. Flip through newspapers and you'll find a politician somewhere, spade in hand, smiling at the camera while planting a tree. The free-wheeling English garden was developed during the eighteenth century as a direct challenge to what had been going on across the Channel. There, landscaping and horticulture reflected the authoritarian monarchies that held sway. Order, regimentation, control, clamping down on natural exuberance were the ways things were done. Whereas enlightened Englishmen bought into the natural look, cultivated by famous practitioners like Capability Brown. They also appreciated the literary and grammatical allusions he used when laying out their estates:

> *Now, there I make a comma and where a more decided turn is proper, a colon; at another part, should an interruption be desirable to break the view – a parenthesis – then a full stop; after which I begin another subject.*

A CAPABILITY
BROWN TOPIARY
COMMA

COFFEEHOUSES

It's a one of the quirks of history that coffeehouses boomed in Britain during the seventeenth and eighteenth centuries when the brew they served up tasted disgusting, judging by contemporary accounts. It was the caffeine kick that turned on customers and kept them coming back for more of the same. By one thousand seven hundred and thirty-nine London alone had 550 such establishments, but these were the exclusive preserve of the male of the species. No booze, no women were the rules of the day. Men congregated where their peers hung out. So, buyers and sellers of fine art and furniture attended Sotheby's and Christie's. Dealers in stocks and shares frequented Jonathan's Coffee House,* which morphed into the Stock Exchange, while shipping interests homed in on Edward Lloyd's place in Lombard Street. However, the first to open wasn't in the capital in fact, but 60 miles down the road in Oxford. That was in 1650. Although there are suggestions that a Cretan member of Balliol College was knocking back a daily cup almost a decade earlier.

A COFFEE HOUSE

---

* **R** The phrase coffeehouse may be repeated, but in this instance a challenge would be ruled incorrect, because Jonathan's Coffee House is a proper noun, and therefore its usage is different to the earlier mention of coffeehouses in general.

COOK'S TOURS

Cruising has come a long way since James Cook's early tours. His descendant, Thomas, a keen advocate of the temperance movement, may have developed his anti-liquor ideas from his globe-trotting forebear who served passengers and crew healthy slugs of lime juice – on the pretext that it would help keep scurvy at bay – plus sauerkraut. They had sandwiches too, a nod to the eponymous peer and Cook's patron. These first trips were also mystery tours. Cook had a vague idea of where they were going and why, but there weren't any maps and no one – European travellers, at least – had ever sailed that way before. Even so Cook's tourists had nothing to complain about except nearly sinking on the Great Barrier Reef and their leader losing it on a beach in Hawaii, where locals thought he was a god, then changed their mind and bumped him off. Arctic weather may have prevented the discovery of the Northwest Passage round the top of Canada, but in warmer climes New Zealand and Australia were added to the list of popular destinations across the empire.

1776

This was a quite a year in British history. Landscape painter John Constable was born. Captain Cook set sail on his third and final voyage. The St Leger was run for the first time at Doncaster. Adam Smith published *The Wealth of Nations* and Edward Gibbon issued volume one of his magnum opus *The Decline and Fall of the Roman Empire*. The Duke of Gloucester, brother of George III, honoured him by permitting the author to present a copy. When the second was finished five years later, the author brought his ducal grace this too. He was received with the cheery greeting, 'Another damned, thick, square book! Always scribble, scribble, scribble!* Eh?!' Yes, 1776 certainly witnessed a momentous 12 months.† I should probably mention a disturbance at a colonial tea party, after which people across the Pond‡ began playing cricket in a base manner, did away with the Queen's English (speech and spelling), and started driving on the wrong side of the road. They called it the Declaration of Independence. We said it was a damn cheek.

---

* **R** If you fancy another fancy piece of Greek, *epizeuxis* (repetition of a word in immediate succession, as seen in 'scribble, scribble, scribble') has been used by both Swifts (Jonathan: 'Silly, silly, silly, you are silly, both are silly, every kind of thing is silly'; Taylor: 'But we are never, ever, ever, ever getting back together'), though no record exists of Taylor suggesting the eating of children.

† **H** Possible hesitation at this point? The player seems to change tack while trying to evade a challenge for deviation. In the opinion of this commentator he gets away with it – just.

‡ **R** *Metonymy*, the use of a word or expression as a substitute for something with which it is closely associated, is another of the rhetorical tricks much favoured to steer away from repetition. In this example, 'Pond' is the metonym for the more prosaic 'Atlantic Ocean'.

Metonymy should not be confused with that other devilishly cunning practice, *mertonymy*, the skill employed by *Just A Minute* wizard Paul Merton to conjure up point-winning displays of verbal dexterity and ingenuity.

IRONBRIDGE GORGE

In days gone by, Ironbridge Gorge in Shropshire was dark and grimy even on a clear day. Its water was polluted with industrial waste and fetid run-offs. The roads were clogged with commercial traffic; the air filled with fumes from belching factories – something had to be done about it, and in 1986 UNESCO stepped in and designated this stretch of the River Severn a World Heritage site. Go there today and the place is scarcely recognisable. Where there were once foundries and workshops, you're tripping over museums and gift shops. Even the locals have bought into the whole idea and traipse about in period dress like extras in a costume drama. The famous cast iron bridge draws visitors like a magnet and there's no denying that it's a hugely impressive structure: all 30 metres of it. Abraham Darby completed his masterpiece in 1779 and they celebrated the event on 1 January two years later by starting to charge people to use it. That marked the beginning of the Industrial Revolution and we've been paying for it ever since.

A DIAGRAM SHOWING HOW
HISTORY REPEATS ITSELF:

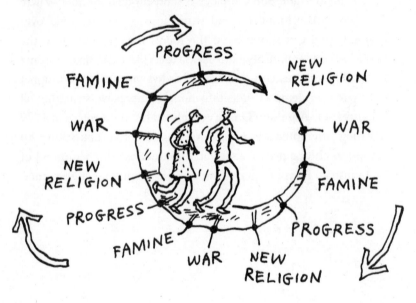

10

The Nelson Touch

EDWARD JENNER

Dr Edward Jenner started vaccinating people in England long before anyone else in western Europe. The French got huffy, just as they did two centuries later when we successfully rolled out COVID-19 jabs way ahead of them. Writing in France at the time, Voltaire noted that Europeans thought we were barking for giving our children smallpox in order to stop them from catching it. You can see his point. However, we Brits took a more enlightened approach to combatting infectious diseases. This is where Jenner entered the picture. Having noticed that milkmaids never got smallpox, he saw a connection with the ailment found in cows and conducted his first trial by rubbing pus resulting from this into a scratch on a young boy. It worked. The little chap was immunised and medicine has never looked back. It's also overlooked* Lady Mary Wortley Montagu (see page 105). She came across the treatment in Turkey, where her husband was ambassador, tried it successfully on her own kids and introduced the idea back home 75 years before Jenner. But as a woman, in the eyes of many, her discovery didn't count.

Being a woman immunises me from getting any credit for the idea of immunisation.

So does being Turkish.

* **R** This almost invites a challenge for the apparent repetition of 'looked'. However, 'looked' and 'overlooked' describe different and opposing actions. While 'looked' points to a purposeful action to behold, or regard, something, 'overlooked' indicates the contrary intention of deliberately disregarding it. Therefore, the one could be taken to be the *antonym* (a word of opposite meaning) of the other, meaning that such a challenge could be dismissed as invalid.

THE SCARLET PIMPERNEL

The scarlet pimpernel (*Anagallis arvensis*) was used in ancient Greek medicine as an antidepressant and in wider European folk medico therapeutics to treat a variety of mental disorders. Generally, it's been regarded as a toxic weed. However, Baroness Emma Orczy and family had good reason to be grateful to it, when royalties from her play and novel, named after this little flower, earned them a very comfortable living. Her plot centres on the daring exploits of Sir Percy Blakeney, an aristocratic waste of space in his day job as a fop about London, but secretly the dashing, courageous saviour of condemned French aristocrats on their way to the guillotine during the Reign of Terror; his signature emblem was this small bloom. In the early 1930s Leslie Howard gave the definitive screen portrayal. He reprised the characterisation in the wartime film *Pimpernel Smith*, the rescuer of thousands of Jews from the Nazis. Apparently, this so inspired the diplomat Raoul Wallenberg from Sweden that he did the same thing for real: saving at least 15,000 using false Swedish passports.*

* Nature imitating art is not something often aired on *Just A Minute*, but the former takes a felicitous lead from the latter in this true and telling anecdote from the Second World War.

BEAU BRUMMELL

Beau Brummell – style icon, fashion guru, promoter of long trousers and influencer par excellence – was the go-to master of elegance and taste in Regency Britain. But as an old-Etonian, sometime cavalry officer, first-class cricketer and Oxford classicist, Brummell was also a proud Englishman, and this did much to influence the manner in which he conducted himself. Many wealthy socialites still sported the foppish fashions they'd picked up on the European Grand Tour: tall, powdered wigs, make-up, silk stockings, you get the picture. Brummell cut against such ostentation, carving out a distinctive pattern of dress as a dandy based on good tailoring, sober fabrics, exquisite linen and polish. He was very keen on the latter, even going as far as insisting on the use of champagne to raise the lustre on his footwear. Coupled with quick wits and a ready turn of phrase, he led the A-listers of his day, notably the Prince of Wales, until their memorable falling out set the Beau on the path to financial and social ruin.

JANE AUSTEN

Jane Austen was an English writer at the time of the Napoleonic Wars when Britain was battling French domination of Europe. Jane Austen took an even-handed view of these events at home, which she saw in the same terms as Brexit a couple of centuries later. Starting with *Sense and Sensibility* she advocated the policy of remaining with what you've got. The argument got more heated in *Pride and Prejudice*, which promoted the opposite point of view: casting everything aside to pursue your own fantasy. Then she rounded off the debate with the eloquently titled *Persuasion*. Her other works hint at the influence she had on the future direction of the Harry Potter stories, particularly when it came to casting the female lead in the films. Is it purely coincidental that the actress who played Hermione Granger also shares her name with two Jane Austen novels (out of a total of less than ten, so over 20 per cent of the entire Jane Austen canon)?* The narratives in question are, of course *Emma* and *The Watsons*.

---

* Jane Austen would perhaps have been this game's greatest player. Not only did she tend to reserve her repetition to *polysyndeton*, which reiterates the link-y words like 'and' and 'her' that don't prompt challenges, as in 'but still they admired her and liked her, and pronounced her to be a sweet girl, and one whom they would not object to know more of'; she was also a mistress of *hypotaxis*, which in plainer speak is a sentence that, like this one, prompts the reader – or indeed the listener, for sentences may be spoken as well as written – when, or indeed if, they will reach an end.

LADY HAMILTON

When Lewis Hamilton marries and is made a lord for services to motor racing his wife will become Lady Hamilton. Until then we need to make do with the Regency pin-up girl who did get hitched to a titled husband and then developed a scandalous *ménage-à-trois* with a national war hero: Admiral H. Nelson.* The latter won celebrated naval victories and lost valuable body parts, but it was his defeat of the French at the Battle of the Nile that brought him and Lady Hamilton together. The strain of conducting their affair in the full blaze of Continental scrutiny, with paparazzi at every turn, drove them to daily mindfulness techniques to reduce stress levels. They found an hour of naval gazing worked wonders. After her lover got a hardy kiss from someone else and died at sea, Lady Hamilton also went to seed before she too passed away. In life, her beau was 5 feet 4 inches tall. His statue on top of the column in Trafalgar Square is 18 feet high. That's Horatio of about 3:1.

---

* Nice blending of contemporary and historical national heroes.

MARENGO AND COPENHAGEN

Marengo was Napoleon Bonaparte's favourite military equine. On the other side of the battlefield the Duke of Wellington sat astride Copenhagen. But through a surreal, though thoroughly delightful, flight of fancy the British Broadcasting Corporation united them in a jolly canter via the airwaves in Radio 4's *Warhorses of Letters*. In the show, Copenhagen is a colt with a crush on his suave Continental pen pal. He signs off his correspondence with a kiss, hoofprint and two repeated crosses. Copenhagen has a stablemate he can't stand: Thunderclap Out of Storm Front by Death to the French. Although Copenhagen quickly downgrades him to a three-letter abbreviation, his envy for his neighbour remains as strong as his ardour for Marengo. The meteorological mount, he laments, has 'a quiff in his mane which he doesn't have to do anything to keep curly'. Marengo is modestly aware of his top knot too. 'I am technically a pony,' he tells his young admirer, 'though I am taller with mine* fluffed up.'

Bonjour, cherie.

Je t'aime.

---

* **R** Students of the Napoleonic Wars will spot the slight change in wording in this statement. To avoid repetition of 'my mane', 'mine' has been used as an acceptable substitute.

WELLINGTON'S BOOT

The Wellington boot was not developed in the capital of New Zealand, nor in the Somerset town of Wellington. It takes its appellation from Sir Arthur Wellesley, 1st Duke of Wellington, British soldier and prime minister, who had a penchant for boots. Wellington liked to leave his stamp on national life and got his cobbler to modify a boot made in the Hessian style, so that Old Nosey could claim the design for himself. Like the Iron Duke's* famous military victories, it was a triumph and, in 1852, Hiram Hutchinson acquired the patent to make Wellington's boots out of the new kind of vulcanised rubber developed by Charles Goodyear. The former set up business in France, where he did a roaring trade selling waterproof boots to people who'd been working the land in wooden clogs for centuries. Both strands of the wellington's history (its eponymous military pedigree and the rural French) came together again on the First World War's Western Front. Sloshing about in waterlogged trenches called for a dry solution and UK manufactures worked round the clock producing 1,185,036 pairs of wellingtons† in the course of the conflict.

---

* **R** Some unnecessary showmanship is displayed in the use of these contemporary nicknames for the Duke of Wellington, when the rules permit the repetition of topic words as often as you would like.

† We have an interesting homophone (of sorts) to ponder in this closing sentence. 'Wellingtons' (the plural) sounds the same as 'Wellington's' (the genitive), but if a well-timed challenge came seven words before the end, you would have to decide if the latter was a repetition of the former. Although the two words have identical sounds, they are, in fact, distinct and therefore different. 'Wellington's' refers to an association with the Duke of Wellington, whereas 'wellingtons' is the plural of the eponym 'wellington' which, as the entry explains, is a type of boot devised by and named after him. Accordingly, the challenge could be ruled incorrect and one would have a second or two left before successfully completing the discourse and gaining a point.

MRS FITZHERBERT

The Mrs Fitzherbert best remembered from the Regency period was the one named Maria, with whom the well-indulged George IV (then the Prince of Ales) became so enamoured that he married her unlawfully and in secret, and they then set up home together in a pavilion in Brighton. However, another Mrs Fitzherbert was also making headlines in the late eighteenth century. In April 1782 London was agog with the news circulating from the West End where John Gay's satirical gem *The Beggar's Opera* was packing them in. The celebrated comedian Charles Bannister, who was blessed with a deep baritone that complimented his muscular frame, was cast to play the heroine, Polly Peachum, in drag. As he sashayed backstage on his way to the wings, one can imagine the cries of 'knock 'em dead'. But, tragically, one night he did precisely that. While most of the audience settled down after greeting his entrance with paroxysms of unbridled glee, the other Mrs Fitzherbert continued laughing so much that she had to leave during the second act and continued to guffaw hysterically until she passed away 36 hours later.

THE INVENTION OF
THE STEAM ENGINE

What is the difference between the first steam engine and the improved one? Get it? Well, you might if you have an interest in physics. If you don't, there's a clue in the opening word I used there. James Watt* was a Scottish engineer who got steamed up over the inefficiency of an earlier model of steam engine that had been designed by the steam engine pioneer Thomas Newcomen in 1711. However, the man named in the previous sentence was not himself the inventor of the steam engine. That honour moved back in time 105 years to 1606, to Spain, where one Jerónimo de Ayanz patented a machine that used steam to pump water from mines. (This was modified a century later by an English inventor called Savory.) But the invention of the steam engine stretches back even further. As early as the first century AD, a Greek enthusiast, Hero of Alexandria, designed a primitive steam turbine. All it did was spin round, but it started people thinking about the potential the steam engine† offered, which the Scotsman mentioned above latched on to for powering the Industrial Revolution.

* Opening with a joke that's also a pun is a hallmark of a skilled player. Not only are people distracted by trying to work out the answer, the subtle manner in which that is given is good for a couple of further lines of diversion, by which stage you're well into your stride and heading strongly for the halfway point.

† **R** This piece cleverly exploits the ruling that permits repetition of topic words. 'Steam engine' is used six times and 'steam' on its own three times and all perfectly within the rules of the game.

THE FIRST BOBBY

The first Bobby, or Peeler to give him his other nickname, of which more shortly, was the first member of London's Metropolitan Police Force. He was called William Atkinson and was the holder of Warrant Number One, issued when the Met* began its work in 1829. It was not a good beginning for the first Bobby nor the crime-fighting agency which employed him, because on their very first day together the first Bobby became the first Bobby to be fired for being drunk on duty. Boozy Bobby bombed, as present-day headline writers might have put it. Unfortunately, the first Bobby was followed 24 hours later by the second Bobby to be shown the door. He was Bill Alcock, next on the official list after the first Bobby, but also the one to immediately follow the first Bobby in being sacked for gross inebriation. Sir Robert Peel must have wondered what he had started, for he was the Home Secretary whose bright idea had brought the country's first professional law enforcement body into being. The two monikers above are cognomens derived from him.†

---

* **R** Some might challenge at this juncture, hoping to seize the topic with a challenge for repetition. However, 'Metropolitan' and 'Met' are orthographically and audibly sufficiently different that a challenge is likely to be dismissed.

† **R** Clever use of synonyms to avoid repetition of 'nickname(s)'.

JOSIE LAWRENCE ON ...
AFTERNOON TEA

It was a day in the year 1840 around mid-afternoon and Anna, the Duchess of Bedford, was feeling peckish. She rang for her butler and said, 'I've got the most awful rumblings in me belly and cannot possibly last until dinner at eight. Ravenous I be! Indeed, quite empty and in need of refreshment, don't cha know. Bring me plates of sandwiches like what that chappie the Earl of Sandwich created, only cut orf the crusts and slice them into the width of a finger. Fill them with butter and thinly sliced cucumber. Yes, that's what I fancy. Oh and cakes! I'll go for a cake or three but the small ones mind, I do not wish to appear too greedy. Yet the idea of a whopping great Victoria sponge fair bursting with strawberry jam and cream pleases me so pop that on the list. Sod it, may as well chuck in some savoury tarts too.' 'Anything else, milady?' enquired the manservant. 'Well, a cuppa tea of course. Now on your way, fool!' Thus the afternoon tea was invented. It soon caught on among the upper-class ladies who would invite each other to their respective and highly impressive homes. There, they would chatter and gossip while drinking copious amounts of tea and stuffing their wealthy gobs.

UNION JACK

Our national banner, the Union Jack (or Union flag to give it its other name), is a classic British compromise; maybe this is why it has no special legal protection, unlike the US Stars and Stripes which is wrapped in protocol and red tape. James I got things going in 1606, when he found himself king of Scotland and England. Their ensigns comprised the emblems of respective saints: the white saltire of St Andrew and the red cross of St George. (Poor old Wales never got a look in, because it was regarded as a principality of its eastern neighbour.) Then along came Ireland in 1801, adding the dark rose-coloured diagonal marking of St Patrick to the mix. The Union Jack's had many uses in its history: from forming part of the standard of Hawaii, to just about covering Geri Halliwell at the 1997 Brit Awards. To be sure of flying it correctly, however, remember: WIDE WHITE TOP or BROADSIDE UP.

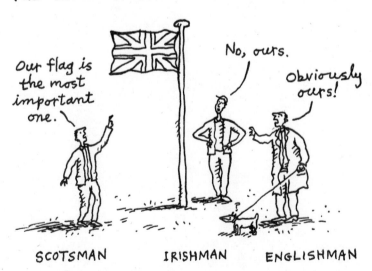

THE UNION FLAG

SCOTSMAN   IRISHMAN   ENGLISHMAN

A SIMPLIFIED TIMELINE:

THEN ⟵⟶ NOW

11

Victoria Was Amused

YOUNG VICTORIA

Young Victoria had a secret – a couple of secrets to be truthful.*
The young queen shouldn't have been Victoria at all, because her
first name was actually Alexandrina – shortened to Drina in her
childhood. In addition, she was only fifth in line of succession when
she was born, but numbers one to four died off, so she succeeded to
the British throne when she was still a teenager, aged 18. It's not
generally known that one of the reasons Young Victoria was often
amused was her tendency to tipple. Beer 'did not agree with her',
apparently, and drinking champagne made her feel 'giddy'. But
offer her sweet ale or negus, a brew like syrupy mulled wine, and
Young Victoria was away – and, in due course, quite a weight. It
was when she topped 9 stone, while standing just 60 inches in her
stockinged feet, that she eased back on the bottle. Mind you, she
can't be blamed for enjoying a drop. She was pregnant for almost
two decades. Her first baby, another young Victoria, arrived just
nine months after she married Prince Albert, and within 17 years
the royal couple had produced four boys and five girls.

* 🄷 This looks like a definite case of hesitation. The hope is to get away with
it by immediately reverting to the topic word; others may be taken in by the
subterfuge and distracted from challenging.

THE INVENTION OF CHRISTMAS

Who would have guessed that Christmas was invented in ancient Rome? Not, as one might expect, in the year zero when the eponymous baby was born into a stable family and wise men came from the east knowing the festive get-together would be well provisioned with fresh livestock. No, the invention of Christmas dates from AD 336, when the first Christmas celebration was held on 25 December, alongside the winter solstice. But for the traditional Christmas as we know it – carols, Christmas cakes, Christmas puddings, Christmas decorations, turkeys and presents – you need to look to Victorian times and Charles Dickens, author of the classic seasonal tale, *A Christmas Carol*. Inspired by the spirit of Jamaican reggae star, Bob Marley, bipolar Ebenezer Scrooge undergoes an overnight personality shift. He ditches his life of solitary reflection and the careful husbandry of natural resources to embrace all the commercial, spendthrift razzmatazz that makes Christmas what it is:* feeding tiny tums, over-indulging larger ones, enduring people you only see once every 12 months, having nightmares that it will all go wrong. We have much to thank the author for.

---

* Useful info: if you're ever discussing 'I Wish It Could Be Christmas Every Day' in *Just A Minute*, the credit, according to the record label, is 'Wizzard featuring vocal backing by the Suedettes plus the Stockland Green Bilateral School First Year Choir with additional noises by Miss Snob and Class 3C'.

THE PENNY RED

The Penny Red was a British postage stamp first used in 1841 to replace the Penny Black introduced the previous year, when the authorities realised that the black ink which franked these adhesive emblems of revenue receipt was hard to distinguish against a background of the same colour, whereas red made it easy to see. Both the Penny Red and its predecessor were the work of the postal reformer Rowland Hill whose favourite wisecrack was one about the letter that got lost in the mail, but he gave up when no one ever got it and concentrated instead of creating a whole new hobby called philately. The Penny Red was printed on sheets of paper containing 240 of the small squares, with 20 rows each containing a dozen Penny Reds. This was very convenient because a purchaser could either buy individual Penny Reds, at one penny each, or exchange a shilling (worth 12 pennies) for a whole line. Big spenders could hand over one pound (twice ten times the value of a strip of Penny Reds) and receive an entire sheet of them.*

---

* Some judicious mathematical phraseology enables this piece to dodge several pitfalls as it approaches the end.

ON THE ORIGIN OF SPECIES

On the Origin of Species was a book published in 1859, which radically changed the way people looked at the natural world and their place in it. As the title page indicates, it introduced readers to the theory that populations develop over generations through the process of natural selection. The author, Charles Darwin, wasn't always an evolutionist, but he became one over time! And his work also showed that biology is the only science in which multiplication means the same as division. There are those who simply don't understand the principles discussed. Dolphins started off as sea creatures, they contend, then evolved to have legs, only to eventually return to a marine environment and lose them. Doesn't that defeet the porpoise? Of course, *On the Origin of Species* has had its opponents since the day it hit the shops. 'If *On the Origin of Species* is true, why are there no crocoducks?' sceptics ask. To which the writer might reply, whether you believe in his thesis or not, one certain thing is that human ancestry is pretty fishy.

ONE OF OUR FISHY ANCESTORS

FLORENCE NIGHTINGALE

Florence Nightingale was a Victorian forerunner of indoor illumination. Hailed as the 'Lady with the Lamp', she shed light on the plight of wounded troops during the Crimean War by showing care and compassion with casual teas. Florence Nightingale was also a pioneer of modern nursing, who encouraged those tending to patients to follow basic hygiene such as washing hands before and after contact with the sick. The results were dramatic and these simple tenets became established practice in preventing the transmission of disease and the prevention of illness. So it does seem surprising that the same lessons had to be banged home time and again during the coronavirus pandemic caused by COVID-19. It was that public health crisis that led to a revival of Florence Nightingale's legacy when, in the 200th anniversary year of her birth, Nightingale hospitals sprang up with incredible speed around the country to provide large-scale facilities to care for victims of this previously unknown respiratory condition.

BIG BEN

To be strictly accurate, Big Ben is the nickname of the largest bell in what used to be called the Clock Tower of the Palace of Westminster, but since Her Majesty's Diamond Jubilee in 2012 has been renamed in her honour. Just to confuse matters, this same structure is also widely referred to as Big Ben. Depending on which Big Ben you're talking about, it either stands 96.3 metres high or weighs 13.5 tons. Work is currently taking place to refurbish the buildings associated with it. This is a huge undertaking and people are working around the timepiece. Big Ben symbolises London the world over. Apparently, the government in Rome is considering installing a similar chronometric device in the leaning edifice in Pisa, so Italians will have the time as well as the inclination. By the way, what has three heads, two tails, eight legs, a beak, a brace of noses, six eyes and one pair of arms? A man riding a horse with a chicken on his head. OK, I 'fess up. I don't know that much about Big Ben.

ANSWER:

cluck.

BOING.

Neigh.

ISAMBARD KINGDOM BRUNEL

Isambard Kingdom Brunel is not just a terrific name, it also belongs to one of the most influential engineers this country has ever produced and a man who was voted second behind Winston Churchill in a poll by the British Broadcasting Corporation in 2002, when people were asked to nominate their 100 top Britons. Brunel's imagination was boundless. Having constructed the Great Western Railway he saw no reason to stop when he reached the Atlantic Ocean and decided that the GWR might as well push its business westwards to America. In order to do this, Brunel designed huge propeller-driven, iron-hulled ships, which changed naval architecture for ever. Bridges, tunnels, docks – Brunel found ways of building them all. As an applied scientist, he saw the world in practical terms. Where an optimist would describe a glass as half full and a pessimist would see it as empty by the same proportion, Brunel would deduce that the vessel was twice as big as it needed to be. That's what made him a genius.

HALF
EMPTY

HALF
FULL

TWICE AS
BIG AS IT
NEEDS TO BE

JUST
RIGHT

THE BIRTH OF THE
LONDON UNDERGROUND

The birth of the London Underground marked a landmark in the history of rapid transport when it opened in January 1863 as the world's very first underground passenger railway. Travellers were conveyed between Paddington and Farringdon in gaslit wooden carriages pulled by steam locomotives. It was noisy, draughty and dirty, but it worked. Today that section of track forms part of the Circle, Hammersmith & City and Metropolitan lines. In my youth I once travelled the entire circumference of the former wearing a paper bag over my head, but at the end of my journey I removed it and saw the light.* The birth of the London Underground led in time to the birth of the nickname by which it is commonly known: the Tube. These days new sections of the Underground are excavated by huge boring machines, which may not enthuse some people, but are absolutely fascinating to those interested in them. At the birth of the London Underground, however, a different construction technique was employed: the cut-and-cover method,† which meant that the original London Underground was only just below the surface.

<hr />

* **D** This personal anecdote could lay the writer open to a challenge for deviation. He may argue that circuiting the Circle Line wearing a paper bag for no purpose other than doing it is not a deviation, but since it has no bearing on the birth of the London Underground deviation it definitely is.

† Indeed, about 200 of the 250 miles of Underground track are overground, which means the network largely deviates from itself.

CHARLES DICKENS

Now we know the truth about George Eliot, Charles Dickens is generally recognised as the greatest male novelist of the Victorian era. The author of such celebrated works as his tome on outdoor cooking *Grate Expectations*, his schizophrenic horror classic *Our Mutual Fiend* and the time-honoured favourite with dog lovers *Edwin Drool*, Dickens was a prolifically creative man in so many ways, not least in his use of language. *The Oxford English Dictionary* credits Dickens with coining 258 new words. Of these, my favourite is 'butterfingers', which first appeared in *The Pickwick Papers* in 1836. He also gave us 'doormat', when used to describe someone walked over by others, 'creeps', as in giving that sensation. Among his other lexical legacies are: boredom, cheesiness, fluffiness, flummox, rampage, clap eyes, slow coach, dustbin, casualty ward, fairy story, egg box and devil may care.*
One expression that has nothing to do with Charles Dickens is the exclamation 'What the dickens!' This 'dickens' is a euphemism for the devil† and the term is first found in print in Shakespeare's play *The Merry Wives of Windsor*.

---

* ℝ Inventive though he is, Charles would not have lasted ten seconds in a game of *Just A Minute*. Consider *A Tale of Two Cities*, from its opening lines ('It was the best of times, it was the worst of times, it was the age of wisdom, it was the age of foolishness …') to the last ('It is a far, far better thing that I do, than I have ever done; it is a far, far better rest that I go to than I have ever known.'). *Bleak House* is ultimately a collection of deviations, while the hesitation at the end of chapter seven of *Edwin Drood* has been going on now for a century and a half.

† ℝ Note the uncharacteristic slip-up, where the otherwise flawless delivery inadvertently repeats the word 'devil'. Worse still, the repetition comes so close to the end, in less than 20 words, a challenger can conclude the subject and gain a point. However, you might feel moved to quote the enquiry from *Edwin Drood*, '… pause and ask thyself the question, Canst thou do likewise? If not, with a blush retire.'

TOWER BRIDGE

Tower Bridge is one of my favourite bridges. It spans the River Thames and the sight of it should fill the breast of any true-born Brit with pride. The bridge dates from 1894 but it was made to look much older so that it would blend in with the nearby Tower of London, from which it takes its name. Fifty designs were submitted, but all but one was rejected. This was the work of Sir Horace Jones and the similarly knighted John Wolfe Barry.* These two Victorian masters of architecture and design were extremely particular about how the construction was carried out. As leaders in their field, they would sit down every day for afternoon tea complete with tablecloth and napkins; it was very civil engineering. Huge quantities of building materials were used in Tower Bridge: over 11,000 tons of steel, approaching ten times that quantity of concrete, 31 million bricks and around one-sixteenth of that number of rivets. The two levered sections in the central span can be raised to an angle of 83 degrees to allow ships to pass. They are called bascules,† after the French word for a seesaw.

Waa hoo!

---

* **R** Nice manoeuvring to avoid repetition of the title 'Sir'.

† Useful info: in 1952, bus driver Albert Gunter found the south bascule under his number 52 was rising. He neither hesitated nor deviated from his route and jumped the vehicle over to the north one. Despite his £10 reward, it's something he never repeated.

SHERLOCK HOLMES

As his assistant and flatmate, Dr Watson, might have put it, 'There's no police like Holmes', for Sherlock Holmes has become probably the best-known detective in the history of criminal investigation. The fact that Sherlock Holmes is a fictional character only serves to reinforce the literary powers of Sir Arthur Conan Doyle who created him. The writer was, like Sherlock Holmes himself, an astute student of human nature and behaviour. Holmes often uses guile and trickery to flush out those suspected of malpractice and the man who chronicled his exploits was not above adopting similar tactics. In a ploy worthy of Holmes himself,* ACD once despatched the same message by telegram to a dozen different men. It read: ALL IS DISCOVERED STOP FLY AT ONCE. According to the sender each of the 12 had fled the country within 24 hours. Sherlock Holmes first appeared in print in 1887 with the publication of *A Study in Scarlet* and his popularity has grown ever since. By the end of the last millennium Sherlock Holmes had featured in over 25,000 stage adaptations, films, television productions and publications.

* **R** Note the crafty manner in which repetition of topic wording, in this case 'Sherlock Holmes', maintains the topic in readers' minds, even though the writer is in fact describing someone else, the author Conan Doyle. A successful challenge could probably be put forward for deviation, but this clever repetition might arouse doubts.

OSCAR WILDE

Those of you who have dipped into earlier portions of this august tome may have read that I am a great admirer of the Irish poet and playwright, Oscar Fingal O'Flahertie Wills Wilde (see page 99). As a boy I was fortunate to meet an old man who had been a friend of Oscar Wilde. He told me that Wilde was such a great conversationalist because 'he could listen as well as talk'. This elderly fellow and I exchanged our favourite Wilde witticisms. Mine was, 'After a good meal one can forgive anyone – even family.' He chose, 'Murder is always a mistake. A gentleman should never do anything he cannot talk about at dinner.' He also told me, 'Wilde always put himself out to be entertaining. He was a delightful person, charming and brilliant, with the most perfect manners of anyone I have ever met. Because of his imprisonment and disgrace he is seen nowadays as a tragic figure. That should not be his lasting memorial. He was such fun.'

TIMELINE SHOWING HOW
HUMAN HISTORY IS
DOING SO FAR...

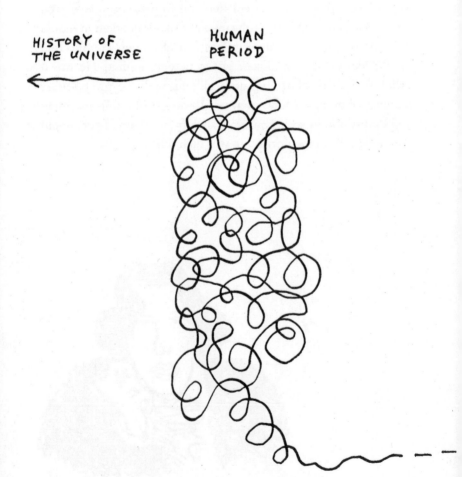

HISTORY OF
THE UNIVERSE

HUMAN
PERIOD

12

A Bag of King Edward's

TO
THE
FUTURE

----------------------------------→

FISH AND CHIPS

Our native cookery has long been the butt of jokes. 'I like both kinds of British cuisine,' runs a typical bon mot, 'fish AND chips.' However, this popular hot dish has spread around the world since it was first generally enjoyed in the UK back in the 1860s. As a forerunner of today's fast-food boom, fish and chips saw massive growth nationwide. Ten years into the twentieth century there were 25,000 fish and chip shops spread across the country; a decade later the number had increased by 40 per cent. During the First World War, fish and chips were one of the very few foodstuffs that were not rationed. The same was true in the second global conflict,* when fish and chips were seen as one of the 'home comforts' and Prime Minister Winston Churchill referred to fish and chips as 'the good companions'. They remained so when peace returned. On one day in 1952, Harry Ramsden's well-known fish and chip shop in the West Yorkshire town of Guiseley sold 10,000 portions.

A BRIEF WRONG TURN...

FISH SHOP CHIP SHOP WIGS

CHIPS
CHIPS
CHIPS

Here's a thought. Why don't we join forces?

Fish and wigs? Brilliant...

---

* The aftermath of the war led of course to an over-reliance on canned goods, thereby to the ubiquity of Spam and so on to a Monty Python sketch the words of which will not be mentioned here.

THE ENTENTE CORDIALE

The Entente Cordiale is regarded as the diplomatic triumph of the reign of King Edward VII, our sovereign during the first decade of the twentieth century. The Entente Cordiale constituted a series of agreements between France and England that were signed in the spring of 1904. They ended close to 1000 years of on–off hostility between the two nations. Topics covered earlier – the Norman Conquest, the Hundred Years War, Joan of Arc, the Battle of Agincourt, the Scarlet Pimpernel, Napoleon Bonaparte, the Duke of Wellington (and their respective horses) – were all consigned to history by the Entente Cordiale, which started a new chapter in Anglo-French relations – a happy fait accompli after centuries of faux pas. Since then our two nations have been brothers and sisters in arms. Inevitably, minor setbacks have made the entente less cordiale at times. Ones that spring immediately to mind include: General de Gaulle's veto to the UK joining the Common Market, London 2012 (not Paris in that Olympic year), the ban on British beef exports, fishermen blocking Channel ports, Brexit. But we have given them Scotch whisky, Kristin Scott-Thomas and *Strictly Come Dancing* (*Danse Avec Les Stars*): and received in return Louis Vuitton luggage, Juliette Binoche and *Dix Pour Cent* (*Call My Agent*). Deuce, je crois – mon brave!

DIRTY BERTIE'S LOVE SEAT

Dirty Bertie was one of the racier nicknames by which Queen Victoria's eldest son was known, although he chose to reign as Edward VII. His prolific appetite for delighting in the 'fair sex' led to other monikers, among them Edward the Caresser. The king's passion for indulgence wasn't restricted to satisfying his carnal desires. Dirty Bertie consumed food and drink to excess and to the point where partaking the pleasures of female flesh became severely hampered by a surfeit of his own. This is where his love seat was such a boon. Custom-made, presumably by royal command, this *siège d'amour* was kept at the famous Le Chabanais brothel in Paris where it served two principal functions, or three as – what one might term – circumstances required.* Dirty Bertie's love seat was designed to ensure maximum gratification for its namesake with minimum effort on his part. It did this by supporting His Majesty's very substantial girth while enabling him to savour an intimate Entente Cordiale with a comely companion, sometimes two, thereby inaugurating a distinctly raunchy Game of Thrones.

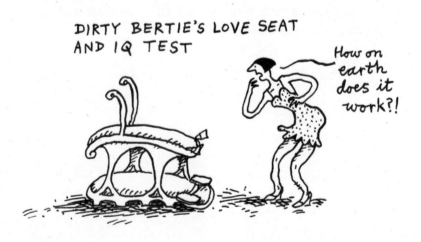

DIRTY BERTIE'S LOVE SEAT
AND IQ TEST

How on earth does it work?!

***

* 🅷 This looks like a rare case of hesitation. Perhaps searching for a decorous euphemism for Edward VII's erotic frolics caused a momentary wavering.

WORCESTERSHIRE SAUCE

Since the end of the nineteenth century Worcestershire sauce has been one of Britain's enduring contributions to world cuisine along with its close neighbour Double Gloucester, its Scottish cousin single malt, Yorkshire pudding, Eton mess (not a euphemism for the current cabinet), Cumberland sausage (no euphemistic references here either), and that heady brew with a kick like a horse: Suffolk punch. The recipe for Worcestershire sauce has always been a matter of speculation since it was first brewed, but it was a firm of apothecaries in the city of Worcester who created the powerful anchovy-based condiment still enjoyed globally. They were Messrs Lea & Perrins, the names under which Worcestershire sauce is still bottled. Its ingredients have been traditionally: spirit vinegar, molasses, sugar, salt, the small member of the herring family mentioned above, tamarind extract, shallots (later onions), garlic, spices and flavourings. Worcestershire sauce brings a tangy, savoury, sweet and salty flavour to everything from the English cheddar cheese sauce to the Australian Oysters Kilpatrick, by way of the Franco-US cocktail Bloody Mary (see page 62).

PETER PAN AND WENDY

At the time of writing, *Peter Pan and Wendy* is the title of an adventure fantasy film that adapts the Coronation Year Disney animation *Peter Pan* into a live-action movie, scheduled for release in 2022. Both are based on J. M. Barrie's 1904 play and novel from seven years later: *Peter Pan; or, the Boy Who Wouldn't Grow Up*, or *Peter and Wendy*, often known as simply *Peter Pan*. Peter Pan and Wendy are the principal characters in the story. Peter is a familiar appellation dating from before biblical times. But the author is widely credited with popularising (if not originating) Wendy.* Other memorable figures in the tale include the pirate skipper Captain Hook, who pretty much sails his ship single-handedly, and the fairy Tinker Bell. She was given the late-addition task of spreading magic aeronautical dust after far too many children had tried to fly from their beds and ended up in hospital. Invited once to comment on the success of his work, its creator replied, 'Some of my plays peter out and some pan out.'

WHY FAIRIES ARE EXTINCT

FAIRY DUST!

DUST FROM 12 DESICCATED FAIRIES IN EVERY TUB!

Sprinkle liberally

---

* **R** He did not, however, name the island which has been *Just A Minute*-d over the years: now usually referred to as Neverland it was, in the original play, 'the Never Never Land', and in Barrie's first draft … 'Peter's Never Never Never Land', though that was never seen again.

THE OLYMPIC GAMES

The modern Olympic Games got going in Greece in 1896 and have gone from strength to even stronger ever since – except in the case of the Winter Olympics sport of tobogganing, which has been going downhill from the start. I have to admit to being ambivalent about the Olympic Games. Asked which was my favourite competition, my answer would be 'Discus'. Aquatic events were enjoyable, but my trial for the diving team was a flop, although I made quite a splash with the judges. I even have my doubts about the original Olympic Games. There are suggestions that ancient Greek athletes used to shave their heads to sprint faster. To me, that sounded like balderdash. So, I wouldn't have been as disappointed as many when the Roman emperor Theodosius closed the original games in around the fourth century AD. Bizarrely, in 1612 in Chipping Campden of all places, some chaps got together and organised what they called the Cotswold Olympick Games. Those ended after 30 years. Even so, the London 2012 Olympic bid made the cheeky suggestion that these forerunners in rural Oxfordshire signalled 'the first stirrings of Britain's Olympic beginnings'. Amazingly, it did the trick.

SCOUTING FOR BOYS

Scouting for Boys was the title given by Robert Baden-Powell to his 1908 manual on Boy Scout training. Its subtitle called it a 'handbook for instruction in good citizenship' and it was here that the author got into hot water as the twentieth century began to take a more enlightened view of how members of society should behave towards, and perceive, one another. For example, he cited the way in which bees organise their hives as a praiseworthy illustration readers would do well to follow. These honey-producing insects, he wrote, formed 'a model community, for they respect their Queen and kill their unemployed'. You can imagine the furore that started! *Scouting for Boys* followed an earlier publication, *Aids for Scouting*, which drew on a guide for military reconnaissance operatives in the field. This became a surprising hit, offering tuition to any boy with a taste for adventure and a sense of civic duty. How many scouts does it take to change a lightbulb? One. But it takes ages because he only does one good turn a day.

EMMELINE PANKHURST

Emmeline Pankhurst was a pioneer of female emancipation in the early years of the twentieth century, particularly the right to vote. She became a leader in the suffragette movement, which conducted a high-profile political campaign promoted by telling messages like this:

Convicts and Ladies, kindly note,
Are not allowed to have the vote;
The difference between the two,
I will now indicate to you.

When once the harmful man of crime,
In Wormwood Scrubs has done his time,
He at the poll may have his say,
The harmless woman never may.

Emmeline Pankhurst was sent to prison herself for conspiracy to commit property damage. In Holloway she went on a series of hunger strikes in which she was joined by fellow internees. The authorities responded with the barbaric practice of force-feeding those who refused food. This, and the fact that their protest was called off during the First World War, helped to win over public opinion and in 1918 British women were allowed to cast their ballots in elections – provided they were over 30 years old.

MARIE STOPES

Marie Stopes was nothing if not controversial. As a campaigner for family planning she brought women relief and possibly an element of pleasure between the sheets. At the same time she was a vocal promoter of eugenics – the distorted philosophy of using controlled breeding to shape the population in the way you would like it to become while erasing the bits that you want to do away with. Six months before the end of the First Word War she published *Married Love*, which was an interesting topic for a woman about to end a conjugal relationship she always maintained was unconsummated. In the absence of the real thing, Marie Stopes theorised about the ecstasy of physical fulfilment. Her book didn't dwell on sexual problems her readers might be coping with. She devoted just one chapter to contraception, preferring to concentrate on the delights marriage could deliver, especially in the bedroom. Some viewed the book as scandalous, but a great many others made it an instant commercial hit. It went through five editions in its first year and established Marie Stopes as a leading advocate for birth control and female rights in general.

THE RACE FOR THE SOUTH POLE

In the race for the South Pole, British explorers thought they were in pole position because they had been trying to reach it more unsuccessfully than anyone else. Different expeditions had struggled to get on in Antarctica, because they all found it difficult to break the ice. Sir Ernest Shackleton managed to walk to within 100 miles of the South Pole but had to turn back because his supplies were running low. Captain Scott did reach the South Pole only to find that he and his companions had lost the race to a team from Norway who cheated by using dogs to pull their sleighs instead of slipping on foot across hundreds of miles of frozen ice and snow, dragging their sledges behind them. Following this huge disappointment, the leader of the party that came second gave up terrestrial adventuring and began a new career as a Human Starfleet Officer on the Starships *Enterprise I* and *II*, aboard which he worked as chief engineer for 30 years in order to obey the command, 'Beam me up, Scotty!'*

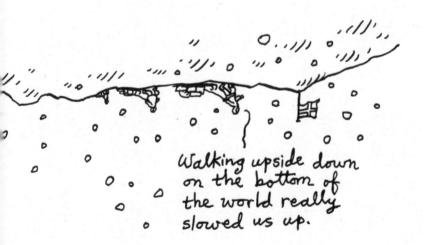

Walking upside down on the bottom of the world really slowed us up.

---

* **R** Another example of the teasing play: provocatively introducing the repetition 'Scott/Scotty' in the final utterance and just as the minute finishes – truly a case of having the last word.

LLOYD GEORGE KNEW MY FATHER

'Lloyd George Knew My Father' is a two-line song sung to the tune of the hymn 'Onward Christian Soldiers'. It goes on and ...* continues in this manner, incessantly repeating the same words (below) until the participants lose the will to live and stop:

Lloyd George knew my father,
Father knew Lloyd George.

Far from being boring, David Lloyd George was one of the most colourful British politicians of the twentieth century even if he did increase taxes during his time as Chancellor of the Exchequer, was fingered for insider trading in top communications' company Marconi's shares and was embroiled in a cash-for-honours scandal, selling titles to boost party funds. It was this malpractice and breach of parliamentary rules that gave rise to the rhyme above, although the lines were open to a saucier interpretation. Lloyd George was a notorious womaniser and the word 'father' was often accompanied by a wink to indicate 'mother', while the verb 'knew' was naughtily interpreted in its biblical sense.

---

* **H** Hesitation! Without a doubt this momentary pause constitutes a breach of one of the trio of cardinal rules. The writer was doubtless seeking to avoid repetition in the phrase 'goes on and on' but this hesitancy would have been enough to let in a successful challenge.

13

The Roaring Twenties

THE CHARLESTON

The Charleston is a carefree dance that came to symbolise the decade after the First World War. Although it has enjoyed revivals in later years, the Charleston became a defining image of the Roaring Twenties, especially in the USA, where it evolved. The Sussex dwelling named Charleston* was equally iconic, but for different reasons. This Charleston was the home of Duncan Grant and Vanessa Bell, leading lights in the Bloomsbury Group of artists and intellectuals. Writing of her Charleston in 1936, the woman painter and interior designer mentioned above commented, 'The house seems full of young people in very high spirits, laughing a great deal at their own jokes ... lying about in the garden which is simply a dithering blaze of flowers and butterflies and apples.' This same joie de vivre characterised the manner in which they would have thrown themselves into the Charleston. You can frolic by yourself, with a partner, or a group, to the Charleston ragtime jazz, in a quick-time signature that has four beats in each measure† and where a quarter note receives one count,‡ plus syncopated rhythms. Or you can enjoy watching others doing it so much better.

* **D** This teasing switch to another subject of the same name could tempt you into challenging for deviation. However, the wording of the title allows for any topic named 'Charleston'. Had it included a reference to the Charleston dance, a deviation challenge might be valid. The key distinction is that it didn't. So, this discourse informs us of two Charlestons that were emblematic of the 1920s, not just one.

† Discussion of rhythm brings to mind the question of which musical forms best and worst fit the rules of *Just A Minute*. Worst is easy: military marching bands and tight funk outfit the Meters. Best is someone enthrallingly unpredictable: Arkansas saxophonist Pharoah Sanders, perhaps, or your niece at a carol concert.

‡ **R** A skilful avoidance of repetition enables this discourse to skirt round the more familiar term: 4/4 time.

THE MYSTERIOUS AFFAIR AT STYLES

Ah, yes, this is the title of a work of fiction written by the great Dame Agatha Mary Clarissa Christie, née Miller, known for her 66 murder mysteries, her 14 short-story collections, and the world's longest-running play, *The Mousetrap*. *The Mysterious Affair at Styles* was originally published in the United States of America in October 1920 and in the UK five months later. It marked the debut for the novelist, her Belgian-born sleuth Hercule Poirot, and the Golden Age of detective writing that followed in the subsequent two decades. *The Mysterious Affair at Styles** also saw its leading man heading away from the one direction down which his career had started, branching into a pleasing new range of cosmetics that drew a *Fine Line* between his previous work and what was to come. Following his baptism of fire in the movie *Dunkirk*, Harry Styles returned to the genre of law enforcement investigation in the film adaptation of *My Policeman*, the book by Bethan Roberts. This writer no doubt drew inspiration from the woman writer whose success with *The Mysterious Affair at Styles* launched the career that established her as the best-selling author of all time, only outsold by the Bible and Shakespeare.

---

* This segue between the 1920s and our present day is deftly handled. The fact that Hercule Poirot paid close attention to his personal toilette is another felicitous association with Harry Styles and his Pleasing beauty brand.

RUPERT BEAR AND WINNIE-THE-POOH

Rupert Bear and Winnie-the-Pooh are probably the two best-known ursine characters in English literature. Rupert Bear entered public life just over a century ago when his employers at the *Daily Express* set him to work in a comic strip to pinch readers from rivals the *Mail* and the *Mirror*. He was hugely popular in the newspaper and later in book form. Purists will tell you that Rupert isn't in fact a bear, but a boy with a bear's head, which is why he has hands and feet rather than paws. Winnie-the-Pooh,* on the other hand, is definitely a bear, inspired by a real bear from Winnipeg and the toy bear belonging to Christopher Robin, the son of the author Alan Alexander Milne. Both Rupert and Pooh achieved international success, although Winnie-the-Pooh holds the distinction of being the subject of the only volume written in Latin ever to make the *New York Times* bestseller list with Alexander Lenard's translation *Winnie ille Pu*. Pooh, of course, is completely at home in the ancient world because he shares a middle name with Alexander the Great.

You mean... I'm not a bear at all...

I'm a mutant boy?!

~~~~~~~
* ▣ The bear's immortal hums are naturally best avoided – unless *you* can think of a synonym for 'tiddly-pom'.

THE BIRTH OF THE BRITISH BROADCASTING CORPORATION

The British Broadcasting Corporation began life as the British Broadcasting Company. That was in 1922 and it was five years later that the word 'Corporation' was adopted, when the British Broadcasting Corporation was established by royal charter. The first general manager was appointed just in time for the initial Christmas schedules. He was a Scottish engineer named John Charles Walsham Reith who cheerfully took on his new job although, in his own words, 'I hadn't the remotest idea as to what broadcasting was.' The British Broadcasting Corporation was the world's earliest state broadcaster and no one knew anything about broadcasting to the whole population of an entire country. They made it up as they went along and the inaugural live public broadcasting in the UK was supplied by a company founded by an Italian named Marconi and featured an Australian singer who was famous for a new way of preparing grilled bread: Dame Nellie Melba. She wasn't British, but Australia had been part of the British Empire so that was all right. And that's how the British Broadcasting Corporation* was born and became the toast of the nation by informing, educating and entertaining us ever since.†

---

* **R** This is a prime example of how one can use up time by legitimately repeating title words. As has been mentioned before, the repetition rule requires you to avoid using the initialism BBC, but this does enable you to deploy the lengthier title of the organisation in full.

† **H** There was a hesitation, though, for obvious reasons, following the broadcast of a Mickey Mouse cartoon on 1 September 1939. Service resumed in 1946 with the same cartoon, setting a pattern for repetition which the Corporation found it enjoyed.

THE GENERAL STRIKE

The General Strike of 1926 should not be mistaken for the military tradition of opening bottles of champagne with a clean swipe across the neck with a cavalry sabre. However, it could be argued that the lifestyle associated with expensive sparkling wine played its part in fermenting the General Strike. This famous industrial action was centred on a dispute between the owners of British mines and the people they employed to extract coal. The former wanted to maintain the comfortable existence that business profits had bought them. In order to do this, they decided to impoverish the livelihoods of the latter by reducing wages and increasing labouring hours. The Trades Union Congress agreed to lend their support in resisting such measures. 'Not a penny off the pay, not a minute on the day' became a national rallying cry and for nine days in May of the year referred to above, 1.7 million workers downed tools. But the General Strike was over in under a fortnight, possibly because Americans didn't join in due to the US ruling: three strikes and you're out.

HOWARD CARTER

Howard Carter was an archaeologist who, quite unintention-ally, started a whole genre of horror films featuring cursing scary maternal figures that went about their terrifying business wrapped in what looked disturbingly like rolls of ancient loo paper. The story began in Egypt where Howard Carter was employed by Lord Carnarvon to see if he could find anything in the Valley of Kings. In November 1922 the local men working for Carter uncovered a buried staircase. When this was cleared, it led to a sealed door. In one of the most dramatic moments in the history of historical research, Howard Carter peered through a small hole and saw 'wonderful things'. What his team had discovered were the burial treasures laid there over 3000 years earlier to accompany the dead ruler Tutankhamun and his mummy to the afterlife. There were containers that once held food prepared by the celebrity royal chef Gordon Ramesses. Carter spotted evidence of other delicacies from Pizza Tut. Although the ones covered in chocolate and nuts were identified as belonging to a different ruler: Pharoah Rocher.*

Mmmm...

---

* **D** Some may conclude that these concluding remarks stray close to deviation. However, you could well argue that what could constitute 'wonderful things' more tellingly than delicacies prepared by a celebrity chef, takeaways from a leading pizza emporium or mouth-watering treats from a major international chocolatier?

JOHN LOGIE BAIRD

John Logie Baird was a Scottish electrical engineer and inventor who created the first live working television from an assortment of everyday bits and pieces including: a tea chest, a hatbox, a pair of scissors, some darning needles, several lenses from bicycle lights, sealing wax and glue. Baird's early experiments didn't always go according to plan. He once gave himself a huge electric shock which sent 1000 volts surging through his body. He survived with only a burned hand, but his landlord evicted him as a danger to life and limb. Baird decided that publicity might help promote his device, but when he went to demonstrate it to the news editor of the *Daily Express*, the poor man was so petrified he yelled to his staff, 'For God's sake, go down to reception and get rid of a lunatic who's there. He says he's got a machine for seeing by wireless! Watch him – he may have a razor.' But within four years of first showing his innovation in public, John Logie Baird began transmitting TV programmes for the Beeb.* Yes, Logie Baird – he was smarter than the average. Think of it, without him there would be no *Bargain Hunt*, or *Homes Under the Hammer*, or *Naked Attraction*.†

---

* **R** The use of 'Beeb' is a calculatedly cunning move. Readers may recall from an earlier entry that the convention on *Just A Minute* is to avoid the repetition of 'B', by referring to the BBC with its full title: British Broadcasting Corporation. That is a wise precaution since BBC repeats the initial initial. However, can the same be said of the nickname Beeb, in which the last letter repeats the first letter and the third letter repeats the second? This raises the thorny question of whether the use of the same letters within a single word constitute repetition. Take the word 'abracadabra' for example. Would it be correct to rule this to as repetition? In the opinion of this commentator that would be very unlikely, since pursuing that logic would render a raft of words ineligible on *Just A Minute*: words such as 'bitter' (which has one repeated letter), 'bassoon' (two repeated letters) and 'bookkeeper' (three repeated letters). And this is when one has only probed as far as the letter 'B', the second of 26. On the basis of this exegesis, 'Beeb' may be bold, but to boycott it would be blinkered.

† **R** Do remember that the 'repetition count' is reset when a new subject arrives, so it is perfectly possible to mention, for example, *Naked Attraction* multiple times, as long as you name it only once per topic.

ALEXANDER FLEMING

Alexander Fleming was another Scottish scientific pioneer, like John Logie Baird. At the turn of this century he was named in *Time* magazine as one of the hundred most important people of the previous one, while a poll conducted by the British Broadcasting Corporation placed him among the same number of the highest achieving Britons in history. The cause of this acclamation and adulation was Fleming's discovery of the world's first antibiotic – penicillin – and it won Alexander Fleming a Nobel Prize. Intriguingly, this all came about as the result of Fleming's habitual untidiness in the laboratory,* where an experiment he left while he was on holiday in the summer of 1928 became covered in mould during his absence. It turned out that this furry growth of minute fungi† had killed a lot of adjacent bacteria. Further investigation revealed that a broth formed from this material contained a substance which destroyed the pathogens that caused infections such as scarlet fever, pneumonia, meningitis and diphtheria. Alexander Fleming's chance medical breakthrough has been described as 'the single greatest victory ever achieved over disease.'

---

* Fleming evidently agreed with Simone de Beauvoir, who sighed: 'Few tasks are more like the torture of Sisyphus than housework, with its endless repetition' – a very *Just A Minute* sentiment.

† **R** Clever formulation to avoid repeating 'mould'.

JACK HOBBS

Jack Hobbs was a famous cricketer in the first half of the twentieth century. Nicknamed 'The Master' and occasionally formally referred to, following his knighthood, by his full name Sir John Berry Hobbs, Jack Hobbs came to personify the style of opening batting that combined elegance and aggression to devastating effect. He was also a renowned fielder, notably at cover point, where his quick hands and devastating bail-high returns to the keeper became the terror of wayward runners between the wickets. When students of the game asked why Jack Hobbs was regarded as a Cinderella of the sport, the reply was that they both knew when to leave the ball. Jack Hobbs played at a time regarded as a golden era when those of every description were welcomed. For example, few other recreational activities accepted the diverse range of body types, which made fine legs, square ones, and short lower limbs feel as much at home in the field as long pins,* the third man and the sweeper.

ELEGANCE
AND
AGGRESSION

JUMP
SKIP
HOP...

---

* **R** All these fielding positions are, of course, identified as being on the leg side of the field and carry the suffix 'leg'. The natural inclination is to use the correct terminology as laid down in the laws of cricket, but to do so would amount to being bowled out in *Just A Minute*. However, this quick-witted writer has metaphorically shown a dead bat to each delivery, before declaring at the end of a successful innings.

WHEN WOMEN GOT THE VOTE

Globally, women initially achieved the right to vote in national or local elections in 1893, when women in New Zealand became the first in the world to cast their ballots. Doing the same with their corsets and stays took longer. The female Kiwi voters were followed by women in Australia nine years later and then by those in Finland and Norway. But British women had to wait until the year in which the First World War concluded before some of them were granted the same opportunity and then they had to be householders aged 30 or over. It was not until the Equal Franchise Act of 1928 that women of 21 and above were able to vote, which finally gave them the same voting rights as men. By the time the greater majority of women got the vote, the staunch campaigner for women's rights, Emmeline Pankhurst, had died, dreading long-haul flights to the end because she always suffragette lag afterwards. Incidentally, women did not get the vote in Switzerland until just over half a century ago, in '71, and in Zanzibar, while women have been able to vote since 2015, their husbands can divorce them automatically if they choose to vote when their husband has told them not to.

ANOTHER WAY OF
LOOKING AT
HUMAN HISTORY...

14

The 1930s

THE FIRST TIMES CROSSWORD

The first crossword was published in *The Times* on 1 February 1930. But it was not the very first crossword to appear in a newspaper. Far from it. That distinction belongs to the Christmas edition of Sunday's *New York World*, published in the year before the outbreak of the 14-18 World War; although the *Times** from that great American city did not print a daily crossword puzzle until the ninth month of the fiftieth year of the twentieth century, making it the last major US paper to adopt that quotidian feature. The editorial board of *The Times* of London took some convincing that a crossword was a good idea. In December '24 the paper decided that the crossword craze in the USA was getting out of hand. Under the headline 'An Enslaved America' it accused the cross-word of being a veritable 'menace because it is making devastating inroads on the working hours of every rank of society'. But its resistance crumbled and six years later the first *Times* crossword appeared. The first clue in the first *Times* crossword (1 Across) reads 'Spread evenly' and requires five letters. The answer begins and ends with two adjacent letters in the alphabet; if you need confirmation, you'll find it a little further on.

---

* **D** This swift and timely switch cleverly dodges a challenge for deviation. The name of the newspaper in the title is given simply as the *Times*, a name by which both these newspapers in London and New York are informally known.

AMY JOHNSON

Amy Johnson was a pioneering pilot, popularised in the British press as 'The Queen of the Air', who set long-distance flying records in the 1930s. Long before the undignified scrum of modern jet travel, which causes some passengers to suffer from terminal sickness, Amy Johnson preferred to fly alone, or in the exclusive company of trusted aviators. At the controls of her aeroplane, she always looked calm. This composed demeanour may have been helped by the large fan spinning at the front. When that stopped was when people started sweating. Amy Johnson made many epic flights. She was the first woman to journey solo by plane from London to Australia and one of the few people to make history at Croydon − a feat she accomplished when she landed there after her record-breaking return airborne trip to South Africa in the year in which the Olympic Games were held in Los Angeles, and the Shakespeare Memorial Theatre was opened at Stratford-upon-Avon.* Over eight decades later, inmates of Hull Prison built a full-size model of her Gipsy Moth. How successful this was in any break-out is not recorded.

* **R** Note the ingenious way in which identifying these memorable events evades the need to supply the date (1932) and therefore avoids repetition of '19', which occurs earlier in '1930s'.

CAT'S EYES

The great and much missed comedian Sir Ken Dodd (see page 226), the sage of Knotty Ash, knew all about the cat's eyes that are such a blessing when driving at night or in poor visibility. He used to tell audiences that the man who devised cat's eyes got the idea when he saw the eyes of a cat reflected in his headlights. If the cat had been going the other way, the comic explained, it would have led to the invention of the pencil sharpener. The innovator behind the original cat's eye, or road stud as it is also known, was a Yorkshireman called Percy Shaw. Travelling after dark once in thick fog, he lost track of where he was going until the eyes of a cat beside the road shone back, indicating where the carriageway and pavement met. This set the motorist thinking and by the end of March 1935 he had designed, patented and begun manufacturing cat's eyes. In the United Kingdom, white cat's eyes denote the centre of single-lane road, or the lines separating one from another on motorways. You shouldn't cross red-coloured cat's eyes, but you can travel over green ones. If you're colour-blind, kindly travel by train.

PICK UP A PENGUIN

Picking up live penguins is something best left to professionals in animal welfare and those engaged in the zoological study of these flightless birds that live in Antarctica. However, the message to 'Pick up a penguin', prefaced by the repetition of the letter 'P' three times, separated by ellipses, became a popular advertising jingle in the eighties, sung by the inestimable if easily imitable *Just A Minute* regular, Derek Nimmo.* The penguin referred to was a biscuit bar filled with chocolate cream and covered with the milk variety of the same confectionery.† It first appeared in shops five decades before the commercial mentioned previously and went on sale in 1932. Its creator was William Macdonald who marketed them under his own brand until that became one under the McVitie's banner, when their companies joined with McFarlane Lang & Co and Crawford three years after the end of the Second World War. Penguin choccie bikkies were well known for the jokes printed on their wrappers. With humorous sallies like this, one struggles to comprehend how that came about: 'Why can't penguins fly? Because they're biscuits enveloped in couverture.'‡

---

* **R** Some other advertising slogans rendered *Just A Minute*-compliant include 'The future's bright: Orange things await'; 'Maybe she's born with it. On the other hand, the reason might be Maybelline'; and 'Have a break; please purchase a Kit-Kat'. All just as snappy, surely.

† **R** Good formulation to avoid repetition.

‡ **R** This is an example of why telling jokes on *Just A Minute* can be challenging and ultimately unsuccessful. In order to avoid repeating the 'covered' and 'chocolate', the 'enveloped in couverture' provides a correct, but less than punchy conclusion. 'Couverture' may be correct as a technical term from the baking and confectionery industries, but it is an example of specialist vocabulary that leaves most other people none the wiser.

MRS SIMPSON

Mrs Simpson, known to her family, friends and fans as Marge, is the wife of Homer Simpson. However, the Mrs Simpson under discussion here is more likely to be another import from the United States. She was called Mrs Wallis Simpson before the pre-Christmas Abdication Crisis of 1936 that led to her marriage to the Duke of Windsor (formerly Edward VIII),* which gave rise to rhymes like this:

> Hark the herald angels sing
> Mrs Simpson's pinched our king.

Although this may not have made her popular in Britain and its empire, *Time* magazine named Mrs Simpson Woman of the Year, the first occasion† this American periodical had ever given that distinction (previously the preserve of male subjects) to a member of the opposite sex. Mrs Simpson's success is all the more impressive since she beat world-famous figures such as the athlete Jesse Owens, US President Franklin Delano Roosevelt, Chinese Premier Chiang Kai-shek, Italian dictator Benito Mussolini and the Pulitzer Prize-winning author of *Gone With the Wind*, Margaret Mitchell.

* Clever to begin with the TV cartoon character of the same name. As a diversionary tactic, it keeps others concentrating on that line of discourse, while you're able to assemble recollections of the person intended by the writer of the subject on the title.

† **R** Nifty avoidance of the repetition of '*Time*/time'.

WHO INVENTED THE JET ENGINE?

What did the propellor say to the jet engine? 'I'm a big fan!' Who invented the jet engine? That's a different question and a subject that has interested aeronautical historians and patent lawyers for more than a century. There is evidence that ideas about jet power were drifting around the ancient world – indeed, we have encountered this principle earlier ourselves. But the first devices we would recognise as jet engines began to appear (if only as blueprints) in the early twentieth century. Inventors from Russia, Italy, France, Japan, Norway and Hungary got in on the act. However, it took an English engineer, Frank Whittle, and a German physicist, Hans von Ohain, to develop jet engines that could actually power aircraft. The former had his original one running by 1937. The latter later admitted that he had studied the legal smallprint protecting this British engine and used elements of its design to build a jet engine of his own. Although he may not have invented the jet engine as such, he was the first to fit one to an airborne whatsit that flew successfully. This was a Heinkel He 178, which made its inaugural flight a week before the outbreak of the Second World War.

THE DANDY

The Dandy was a British children's comic that began in December 1937 and reached its heyday a couple of decades later with weekly sales of two million. *The Dandy* differed from competitors through the use of speech balloons instead of captions displayed beneath the illustrations. The longest running cartoon strips within the colourful illustrated journal featured the cow-pie-consuming Desperate Dan and Korky the Cat, both of whom debuted in the first edition. That cost two pence back then, and the price included a free whistle. The outbreak of bovine spongiform encephalitis* in 2001 forced the former to give up his favourite food for the duration of the agricultural infection. Four years earlier he had temporarily retired to spend time with pop group the Spice Girls. But fans worldwide were enraged and his Dundee publishers, DC Thomson, had to admit it was a publicity stunt in advance of *The Dandy's* sixtieth anniversary. The feline character commandeered the front page of *The Dandy* for 47 years almost without interruption. More of a *Beano* than a *Dandy* man myself, I was nonetheless saddened by the publication's eventual demise on 4 December 2012, at the time of its seventy-fifth birthday.

---

* Here is another example of how using full wording rather than initials (BSE in this case) helps you spin out time while also momentarily bamboozling others while they try to work out what bovine spongiform encephalitis actually is.

THE JARROW MARCH

There was no cow pie for those taking part in the Jarrow March, and little enough of even basic foodstuffs. Although there had been a number of 'hunger marches' to London in the years following the First World War to protest against unemployment and the privations endured by large sections of the people living in run-down industrial areas of Britain, the Jarrow March of October 1936 has come to be seen as a key event in the move towards the social and economic reforms that were introduced in the second half of the twentieth century. Jarrow had developed around its shipyard on the River Tyne, but like many communities reliant on maritime construction, it suffered severe hardship when its principal source of work was closed. Encouraged by local politicians and civic leaders, ten score* of men set out to walk from Jarrow, aiming to arrive in the capital at the start of the new parliamentary session. They carried with them a petition with 11,000 signatures requesting the government to re-establish viable industry in Jarrow. The march covered 291 miles and lasted a day over three weeks.

* ℞ Nice archaism employed to get around repetition in '200/291'.

SEEING THE LOCH NESS MONSTER

Seeing the Loch Monster is a phenomenon restricted to Scotland – because that's where you will find Loch Ness, that country's second largest lake – and, as some sceptics contend, may depend on the quantity of Scotch consumed prior to any sighting. But they may be conflating the monster with a campaigner against strong liquor, the American Prohibition agent, Eliot Ness, who led the team that went after bootlegging mob monster Al Capone.* Although there had been sightings of the Loch Ness Monster, or Nessie as it is known in folklore, over many centuries, it was an account published in 1933 that really caught public imagination. The 'witnesses' to this famous event described 'a most extraordinary form of animal' as wide as a road. The creature was, 'The nearest approach to a dragon or pre-historic animal that I have ever seen in my life,' with 'a long neck, which moved up and down in the manner of a scenic railway'. The monster's body was said to be 'fairly big, with a high back, but if there were any feet they must have been of the web kind'. If you don't believe it, go to the Highlands and look yourself – plenty do! Say it, see it, sorted.

---

* The orthographic play on 'monster/mobster' is amusing and displays the kind of verbal agility admired by keen followers of *Just A Minute*.

PEACE FOR OUR TIME*

'Peace for our time' was a phrase used by British Prime Minister Benjamin Disraeli in 1878, when he returned from the Congress of Berlin, which had been convened to stabilise the political and security situation in the Balkans. Sixty years later it was repeated by the then leader of the government Neville Chamberlain after he too had come back from Germany following an attempt to secure long-term peace in Europe. On this occasion the UK premier believed he had reached an agreement with chancellor Adolf Hitler that their two countries would maintain a non-aggressive coexistence, although the Second World War would break out less than 12 months later. 'Peace for our time' is often misquoted as 'Peace *in* our time', which was the title of a play written by Noël Coward soon after the end of the global conflict above.† His drama depicts an alternative history in which Axis forces occupy this country, and was based on the sufferings of French citizens during the Occupation of France, in which the playwright took a close interest. The story of the fellow caught short in shrubbery is called 'Piss in our Thyme' and is about something else altogether.

* 'Peace for our time' may not always be applicable when tackling crossword puzzles. If the solution to the first clue in the first crossword published in *The Times* still eludes you, it is 'smear'.

† **D** This part of the discourse strays close to inviting a challenge for deviation. However, the similarity of the two phrases and their close association with the Second World War may well deceive others into concluding that the subject matter is a valid adjunct to the subject at hand.

ALL YOU NEED TO KNOW!
THE HISTORY OF THE
ENTIRE UNIVERSE...

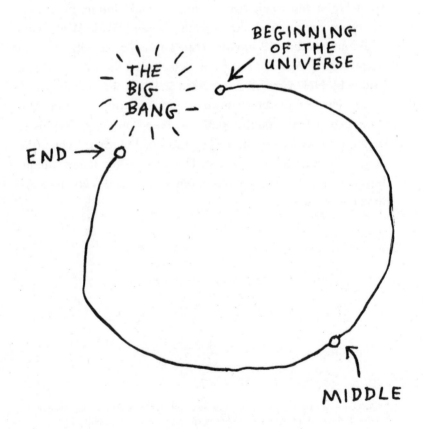

15

Going to the Pictures

THE TALKIES

The talkies we're discussing here were a form of cinematic entertainment developed in the late 1920s, not *The Talkies*, which was the title of the second album released by Irish post-punk and noise musicians Gilla Band. Talkies, or talking pictures as they were called in the USA, were developed in Hollywood. But the enthusiasm for them soon spread and filmmakers in Europe became hooked on the new craze. The talkies marked the end of the era of silent films, but there were no final words to mark their passing. Instead, dialogue and soundtracks added new dimensions to going to the flicks, although producers kept clear of jazz and classical music at first; there was too much sax and violins for their liking. The first European-made dramatic talkie to be truly successful was the thriller *Blackmail*. This was an all-British production directed by Alfred Hitchcock, who was approaching 30 at the time. He made a cameo appearance, as he would continue to do in many of his later productions. When you want to take your dog for a walk, you cry 'Walkies!' When you want to go the cinema, you shout 'Talkies!'

CHARLIE CHAPLIN AND CARY GRANT WERE BRITISH

It's absolutely true, Charlie Chaplin and Cary Grant – two of Hollywood's biggest stars from its golden age – were both British. Charles Spencer Chaplin was born in London in 1889 and Archibald Alec Leach (he became Cary Grant at the start of his movie career when he was 27) came into this world in Bristol 15 years later. It was seeing Charlie Chaplin performing live on the music hall stage with the Fred Karno troupe when he was five that inspired young Archie to pursue a career in showbusiness. For his part, Charlie Chaplin travelled to America to appear in vaudeville and it was there that he was scouted for the movies. Both actors established themselves as accomplished comics: Chaplin for his trademark tramp character and Cary Grant for his fine turn as a master of slapstick – his status as the urbane leading man of romantic comedies came subsequently. But ties to their British roots remained. Charlie Chaplin is remembered by a statue in Leicester Square, Cary Grant by one in his home city's harbourside.

C. C.   C. G.

BRIEF ENCOUNTER

Brief Encounter may sound like a furtive skim through an Ann Summers catalogue but it is in fact the title of a classic of British cinema, the 1945 film written by Noël Coward, directed by David Lean, and starring Celia Johnson (sister-in-law of James Bond creator, Ian Fleming) and Trevor Howard. At the turn of the twenty-first century, the organisation that promotes and preserves film-making in the UK ranked *Brief Encounter* as the second greatest British movie of all time, topped only by *The Third Man*, in which the male lead in *Brief Encounter* also took a starring role. The plot of *Brief Encounter* is based on a one-act play by the same writer, whose voice is heard in *Brief Encounter* making public address announcements at the railway station, which is a key location. The transport hub chosen for shooting is at Carnforth in Cumbria, which was selected for being far away from large urban centres and therefore was not restricted for night-time camera work by wartime blackout regulations – *Brief Encounter** having been made in the months before the end of the Second World War.

---

* **R** Clever manipulation of the rules enables multiple repetition of the subject, with the words *Brief Encounter* being repeated five times with complete impunity.

HAMMER HORROR

Hammer Horror is the name given to the range of horror movies made by the British company Hammer Film Productions Ltd based in London.* The company started in business in 1934 and specialised in the Gothic and fantasy genres, which were especially popular in the second half of the twentieth century. I enjoyed Hammer Horror features so much that I had a go at writing a horror script of my own. I chose a subject close to my heart and centred the plot on a sentient pen. It proved to be the perfect choice and the screenplay practically wrote itself. These days I'm more squeamish and find watching horror pictures less scary on my iPhone – I have it set on Do Not Disturb. Hammer Horror pulled in all the favourite characters from horror fiction and folklore. Frankenstein blundered about lurching from one bodybuilding contest to the next. Dracula made regular appearances after revamping his castle and staking his life on the next bite. And the Mummy ended up in stitches after making the grave mistake of lying in the wrong coffin.

---

* **R** If discussing Hammer films, on no account name more than a couple. It may have taken them 20 years to make their first vampire flick, but *Dracula* was followed by *The Brides of Dracula, Dracula: Prince of Darkness, Dracula Has Risen from the Grave, Taste the Blood of Dracula, Scars of Dracula, Countess Dracula, Dracula A.D. 1972, Count Dracula and his Vampire Bride* and *The 7 Brothers Meet Dracula*.

MY FAVOURITE CARRY ON ...

My favourite *Carry On* film is probably *Carry On Cleo* starring *Just A Minute*'s very own Kenneth Williams as the character Julius Caesar, in which part when he is assassinated he comes up with one of the greatest lines in all cinema: 'Infamy! Ditto! They've all got it in for me!'* I agree, without the repetition of that first six-letter word it doesn't have quite the right ring to it, but in the movie, as far as I'm concerned, it's up there with 'Frankly, my dear, I don't give a damn,' and 'You were only meant to blow the bloody doors off.' This *Carry On* was the tenth in the series, I think, and made in 1964 as a spoof of the epic *Cleopatra* that had been filmed with Elizabeth Taylor in the title role and Richard Burton as Mark Antony – that was Sid James's part in the *Carry On* version. The Hollywood blockbuster cost millions to make and its stars were paid more than a million each. By contrast, Kenny W told me that he never earned more than £5000 for any of the 31 *Carry On* films and only three thousand five hundred for this one, my favourite.

---

* **D** If you were to claim that Caesar's actual last words were 'Et tu, Brute', you'd risk deviation as (a) in the play, he adds, less impressively 'Then fall, Caesar' and (b) in real life, he was probably too busy bleeding to say anything quotable.

THE RAILWAY CHILDREN

The Railway Children is a novel by E. Nesbit, published in 1906 and made into a memorable British film in one thousand nine hundred and seventy. The novel had been through television adaptations and in the most recent of these, aired two years before the big screen version, Jenny Agutter had been cast to play the part of the eldest child in the tale, a character she reprised in the movie. The actress was 17 at that time, whereas Sally Thomsett (aged 20) was given the role of her 11-year-old sister, on condition that she didn't divulge her real age, and that she was never to be seen smoking or drinking while they were shooting. With a screenplay by Lionel Jeffries, who also directed, *The Railway Children* has been described as perfect family entertainment. Released at a time when cinema audiences were enjoying increasingly permissive productions and storylines, *The Railway Children* managed to retain its period charm without overt sentimentality and I just love it, which is why I'm very apprehensive about the forthcoming sequel, *The Railway Children Return*. But who knows? Look at *Richard III* and *Paddington 2*. Sometimes a follow up can be better than the original.

FOUR WEDDINGS AND A FUNERAL

Four Weddings and a Funeral was one of those marvels of the British cinema: a film that was a huge global success almost by chance. Shot in six weeks, with a budget of under three million pounds, it became the highest grossing UK movie until that point, when worldwide takings exceeded well over 81 times what it cost to make.* *Four Weddings and a Funeral* made its leading man, Hugh Grant, an international star. He had been considering giving up acting before his agent sent him the script. Seventy actors were auditioned to play Charles and initially his casting was resisted on the grounds that he was too good looking. Money was tight on *Four Weddings and a Funeral*. Andie McDowell (who played the principal love interest) took a 75 per cent cut in her fee, receiving $245,000 as a down payment, although that would increase more than 12-fold when *Four Weddings and a Funeral* became the massive hit it is. Most of the extras were unpaid, although former Home Secretary Amber Rudd managed to earn a modest sum as the production's 'Aristocracy Co-Ordinator'.

* **R** This mathematical formula displays a clear grasp of the pitfalls repeating numbers can present, but it calls for digital dexterity as well as quick thinking.

TRAINSPOTTING

Trainspotting might be mistaken for a sequel to *The Railway Children* (see page 185) but it most definitely isn't – anything but. For a start, travel by train barely features in it; *Trainspotting* comes from the jargon of heroin addiction which is a central theme in the picture and the novel by Irvine Welsh on which it is based. However, the strong Scottish realism in Danny Boyle's production meant that some of the dialogue had to be given subtitles for release in America so that audiences there could make sense of what was being said. The movie was pitched as Blighty's answer to *Pulp Fiction* and as such it achieved huge international success. Even with limited release, it still made $16.4 million in the USA. *Trainspotting* was the highest grossing British film of 1996 and at that time set the record as the biggest earner ever. *Empire* magazine summed up *Trainspotting*'s success as 'something Britain can be proud of and Hollywood must be afraid of. If we Brits can make movies this good about subjects this horrific, what chance does Tinseltown have?'* My point exactly.

---

* **R** Clever use of a direct quotation means that you can take up valuable seconds repeating someone else's words when running out of your own.

THE BEST BOND

When it comes to the best bond, the subject presents a number of opportunities. One could focus, for instance, on the adhesive properties of various brands of super glue. Those with an eye on investments might select the best bond from a portfolio of financial products. Taking a metaphysical approach could lead to a discussion of which kind of bonding delivers the best bond: marital, parental, fraternal, sororal?* However, many would immediately hit on the 007 character created by Ian Fleming and named by him, according to some accounts, after an American ornithologist: James Bond. This Bond is best known through his film portrayal and here his relationship with birds was compromised by a shallow exploitation of gender stereotypes. Judged on that basis, the early screen Bonds fall short of being 'best', though in my book Roger Moore was the best Bond because he appeared never to take himself or the character too seriously. Half a century on, it took screenwriter Phoebe Waller-Bridge to produce a Bond that present-day audiences might consider to be 'the best', even if Daniel Craig has grey hair in his last outing because he had 'No Time to Dye'.

* **D** This is actually a completely valid discussion of the options presented by the wording of the topic. Good play; good strategy.

BEND IT LIKE BECKHAM

Bend It Like Beckham is a football technique perfected by the former Manchester United and England player David Beckham, whose career established him as a master of dead-ball kicks, particularly when it came to striking a stationary one so that it curved past a wall of defenders before entering the goal. However, Beckham only appears at the very end of *Bend It like Beckham*. There's plenty of soccer action but none of it features him, nor his wife Victoria, even though the plot is centred on women's footie.* It is, though, the highest grossing footballing film ever made and was number one in British cinemas for three weeks after its release. One of its more remarkable accolades was its appearance in North Korea, where an edited version was screened on Boxing Day 2010. Apparently, this was intended to celebrate the tenth anniversary of diplomatic relations between that country and the UK and it made *Bend It like Beckham* the first Western-made movie to be shown on television in that heavily controlled part of the world.

* **D** Good tactics deployed in this clever example of how you can keep going for half the allocated time on a subject that is *not* specifically the one earmarked, but is still sufficiently related to that topic to avoid a challenge for deviation.

THE
PAST
←

THE
PRESENT

THE
FUTURE
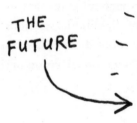

unless there's
No future!

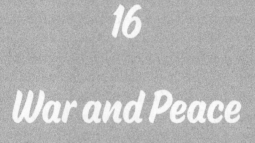

16

War and Peace

MR CHURCHILL'S CIGAR

Ah, this is a reference to Britain's wartime leader and his favourite smoke. 'Mr Churchill's cigar' came to symbolise the national spirit of indomitable resistance and fortitude that he himself personified as British prime minister during the dark days of the Second World War. Winston Churchill adored cigars, almost as much as he loved Pol Roger champagne and Johnny Walker whisky (Red and Black). 'Smoking cigars is like falling in love,' Churchill observed. 'First, you are attracted by its shape; you stay for its flavour, and you must always remember never, ever* to let the flame go out!' Accounting for his prodigious appetite for the cigar, he explained, 'I drink a great deal,† I sleep a little, and I smoke cigar after cigar. That is why I am in two-hundred-percent form.' His favourite brand of cigar was Romeo y Julieta, but he bought other marques as well – purchasing boxes by the dozen. His country home, Chartwell, had a storage area for up to 4000. Churchill-size cigars, seven inches long by 47 ring gauge, were synonymous with the great man – just as cigarettes called Holy Smokes were with another, more controversial, world leader at the time: His Eminence the Pope.

---

* **R** The actual quotation repeats the word 'never', but to avoid repetition a lightning-quick adjustment dropped the initial letter to avoid repetition. Well played. Churchill is perhaps best known for anaphora ('we shall fight them …'), but was not averse to a spot of epizeuxis (saying the same word until people start listening), as in his 1941 speech to the boys of Harrow: 'this is the lesson: never give in, never give in, never, never, never, never.'

† **D** According to historian David Lough, the Churchill household annually spent £90,000 (in today's money) on wine, so this is no deviation, though the intake may have caused the man himself to deviate.

VACKEES

'Vackees' was the name given to children evacuated from their homes in densely populated areas of Britain during the Second World War. Even before the conflict was official the government started moving over three million residents of the nation's cities to smaller communities around the country. Famous vackees included later entertainment stars such as Michael Caine, Roger Moore, Michael Aspel, Bruce Forsyth and indomitable *Just A Minute* veteran Dame Sheila Hancock. Their memoirs all include touching tales of their childhood wartime experiences. Many urban youngsters had never left home before and going to rural areas in particular was as much of a shock as having to say goodbye to their parents. But it wasn't all bad. If it hadn't been for the vackees we might never have had C. S. Lewis's fantasy series *The Chronicles of Narnia*. These begin with *The Lion, the Witch and the Wardrobe* in which the four Pevensie offspring – Peter, Susan, Edmund and Lucy – are sent out of London in 1940 to escape the arial bombardment called the Blitz. Their new rural home is a large house belonging to Professor Digory Kirke, who has the eponymous piece of furniture in his attic.* And so the story begins ...† and hopefully my minute ends.

Welcome ...

---

* **R** And in an echo of Churchill's epizeuxis just mentioned, Chapter Five ends with what would today be called a life hack: 'you should *never never* shut yourself up in a wardrobe'.

† **D** Possible digression leading to a challenge for deviation? It's a moot point and a tricky ruling. There is no denying that the C. S. Lewis characters are 'vackees' and since the topic title does not specify which vackees are to be spoken about, it might be difficult to support a challenge for deviation.

DUNKIRK

Dunroamin is the name of my Auntie Agnes's retirement cottage in Dungeness. Dunkirk is a town on the coast of northern France, which has the country's third largest harbour. In May 1940 an onslaught by invading German aircraft and fast-moving armies forced four-tenths of a million British and French troops to retreat to Dunkirk, where complete defeat looked likely until the so-called 'miracle of Dunkirk' brought about the evacuation of 338,226 of them in an armada of vessels ranging from naval assets* to the famous 'Little Ships' comprising small pleasure craft and those used for fishing. The late fifties movie *Dunkirk*, starring John Mills, Richard Attenborough and Bernard Lee, was shot in and around Rye in East Sussex and cost less than £400,000. Six decades later Christopher Nolan's *Dunkirk* was made using many of the actual settings in Dunkirk and a complex time-twisting formula that kept audiences riveted trying to work out what was happening and when. This *Dunkirk* had a production budget 375 times greater than its predecessor, but it became the highest grossing Second World War motion picture ever made. The soundtrack was a bit too loud for my liking.

---

* **R** Nice use of defence terminology to avoid repetition.

THE BATTLE OF BRITAIN

'Don't mention the war!' was the excellent advice Basil Fawlty famously gave his staff when some German guests were staying at his hotel. It's difficult to do when talking about the Battle of Britain – fought during the summer of 1940. Defending these islands at the time were the 'few': pilots of fighter aircraft in the RAF and Fleet Air Arm. Opposing them was a greater number of aviators of the German Luftwaffe whose task it was to win supremacy of the skies, either to launch an invasion of Britain or bring about an armistice. For much of the conflict victory hung in the balance and often depended on the performance of individual participants. One brought down half-a-dozen Messerschmidts, ten Heinkels and seven Dorniers. He was the worst mechanic on the enemy side. The Battle of Britain became so called after a famous speech in the House of Commons given by Prime Minister Winston Churchill on 18 June of the year in question when he said, 'What General Weygrand called the Battle of France is over. I expect that the battle of Britain is about to begin.' He concluded with the memorable words, 'If the British Empire and its Commonwealth last for a thousand years, men will still say, "This was their finest hour."'

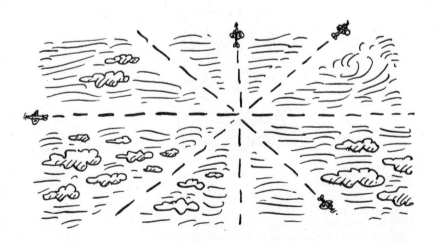

WOOLTON PIE

Woolton pie is a culinary classic made without meat that took its name from Frederick James Marquis, 1st Earl of Woolton, a businessman, statistician and all-round good egg who was appointed Minister of Food in 1940. Not an easy job, but history reckons he did it rather well. Lord Woolton is the dude who introduced rationing in Britain to ensure that supplies could be sustained. Certain products such as decent animal flesh and eggs were very hard to come by. So Woolton encouraged the nation to live off simpler, but still nutritious, fare and this was how the Woolton pie originated. Francis Latry, Maître Chef de Cuisine at the Savoy Hotel, devised the pie to make use of whatever was available: for instance diced and cooked potatoes (or parsnips), carrots, cauliflower and maybe turnip. This was topped by a spud pastry and grated cheese, and served with a vegetable gravy. The eponymous recipe was so popular with its namesake that Woolton ate his humble pie morning, noon and night. Although consuming too much cake was a sin of gluttony, especially in wartime, eating an excessive quantity of pie was all right because the sin of pi* is zero.

No animals
harmed in
the making
of this pie!

---

* **R** Some nice trickery at play here, blending Euclidian geometry with wartime rationing. It may also be intended to disguise the repetition of 'sin', coming so close to the end that the combination of a mathematical constant with a vegetarian staple may distract potential challenges for long enough to squeeze in the last four words without being detected.

THE FULL MONTY

Mention *The Full Monty* and I can't resist retelling the true tale of the time I found myself at the Royal Variety Performance in the presence of Her Majesty The Queen and His Royal Highness The Duke of Edinburgh.* Glancing down the programme towards the end of the first act, Prince Philip became animated when he read that the finale was an item entitled *The Full Monty* and assumed we were about to be treated to a fitting tribute to the great wartime general, Field Marshal Montgomery, victor at the Battle of El Alamein. Tugging a forelock, I murmured, 'I think you're under a bit of a misapprehension, sir. *The Full Monty* is actually a show about a male striptease group, like the Chippendales, you know – er,† unemployed firemen, then they come on and strip off ...' HRH was still absorbing this when these strapping lads marched onto the stage and didn't leave until they had bared their all. As we know, the problem with naked dancing is that not everything stops when the music ceases. I sat aghast. Our sovereign lady gazed on the scene totally unfazed. Her consort whispered to me: 'You needn't worry. She's been to Papua New Guinea – and seen it all before.'

---

* Titles are a handy way of using up some seconds, but longer titles are riskier, as with the 25th word of the official one here: Elizabeth II, by the Grace of God, of the United Kingdom of Great Britain and Northern Ireland and of her other realms and territories Queen, Head of the Commonwealth, Defender of the Faith.

† **H** Hesitation! No question about it. The hesitation occurred during the recitation of reported speech; in other words recalling something said on another occasion and – this is the key point at issue – reporting it verbatim, as delivered. To carry the full drama, or humour, of the moment accurately and with conviction requires a pause in the reported delivery, indicating a moment (that word again) to reflect how to phrase what had to be conveyed to the monarch and her husband. Had the pause been omitted, the recounting of this delightful episode would be both inaccurate and less entertaining. And, since accuracy and entertainment are two of the staples of *Just A Minute*, you might well overlook the hesitation. But it's a hesitation. No question about it. (And that is a repetition.)

WE'LL MEET AGAIN

'We'll Meet Again' was a British song released in 1939 and sung by Vera Lynn, which became one of the signature tunes of the Second World War. The lyrics go (something) like this:

> *We'll meet again,*
> *Don't know where, unsure when,*
> *But I'm sure we'll meet again*
> *Some sunny day.*
> *Keep smiling through,*
> *Just like you always do,*
> *Till the blue skies drive the dark clouds far away.*
> *So will you please say hello*
> *To the folks that I ken,*
> *Tell them I won't be long.*
> *They'll be happy to hear*
> *That as you saw me go,*
> *I was singing this song.*
> *We'll meet again,*
> *Not certain of the location,*
> *Unclear too of the timescale,*
> *But I am confident we'll meet again,*
> *During an unclouded twenty-four hour period.**

'We'll Meet Again' proved to be so popular, it became the title for a mid-war film starring its singer. It also featured at the closing sequences of Stanley Kubrick's movie *Dr Strangelove*, when it was played over footage depicting a global nuclear holocaust.

---

* Anyone familiar with this song will immediately spot that some of the lyrics have been 'adjusted' to conform to *Just A Minute* strictures. And anyone familiar with the show will enjoy how we've managed to occupy most of the minute by simply delivering the words of the song, albeit with some small modifications.

HMT EMPIRE WINDRUSH

This is the name of a vessel with an extraordinary and at times grim history. HMT *Empire Windrush* stands for His Majesty's Transport *Empire Windrush* – a passenger liner that sailed between 1930 and '54 under both German and British flags. The ship was launched in Hamburg and originally named the *Monte Rosa*. When Adolf Hitler came to power, she was used to spread Nazi propaganda in a series of voyages at home and overseas. The Second World War saw her serving as a troop carrier in Norway, but also as a transport taking Jewish people from that occupied country to concentration camps in mainland Europe. At the end of the global conflict she was seized as a prize of war and renamed HMT *Empire Windrush*. Three years later HMT *Empire Windrush* called at Kingston, Jamaica, to collect servicemen on leave. They were joined by just over 800 Caribbean citizens who wanted to emigrate to the UK under the terms of the British Nationality Act which was going through parliament at that time. Those who decided to settle here permanently, and others who followed them, became what is referred to as the 'Windrush Generation'.

GEORGE ORWELL'S 1984

George Orwell was the nom de plume of English writer Eric Arthur Blair – no relation to Tony of that name, a sometime British prime minister, or Lionel, his dad. The novel *1984* was the last published during the author's lifetime when it appeared four years after the end of the Second World War. It is a dystopian tale of life under a repressive totalitarian regime modelled on the Nazi one led by Adolf Hitler and the Soviet system under Joseph Stalin. George Orwell's *1984* introduced a number of expressions and turns of phrase which have become widely used in our language: terms like Big Brother, Thought Police, Newspeak and doublethink. His work also gave rise to the adjective 'Orwellian'. As *1984* nears its finale, the principal character, Winston Smith, is taken to Room 101, a torture chamber in the basement of the Ministry of Love, where victims are confronted by 'the worst thing in the world'. Orwell had spent tedious meetings in a room with this appellation in Broadcasting House. The Beeb* used this as the title for a comedy television programme – initially hosted by our very own Paul Merton – in which guests were invited to consign their pet hates to the eponymous boudoir.

I think therefore I am...

You're under arrest.

For thinking AND being yourself.

---

* A discussion of the acceptability of Beeb on *Just A Minute* can be found earlier – if you haven't absorbed it already.

THE END OF RATIONING

The end of rationing in this country came after the conclusion of the Second World War, but it took 107 months from the ceasing of hostilities for all rationing to be brought to an end. That happy day was 4 July 1954 when the rationing of meat including bacon came to an end on the stroke of midnight. Hooray! The UK had endured rationing for 14 years and rationing existed for more than foodstuffs. Petrol, clothes, furniture, sweets and chocolate were all rationed and people had to eke out supplies controlled by ration books. A black market existed for these items and some people hung onto the paperwork for deceased relatives and continued to draw their rations. One of the most distinctive markers of the end of rationing was in the New Look of women's fashion spurred on by Christian Dior, whose voluminous calf-length skirts replaced fabric-conscious wartime designs. Although not everyone was wowed. Coco Chanel dismissed her rival's acclaimed collection as, 'Clothes by a man who doesn't know women, never had one, and dreams of being one!'

ALAN TURING

Alan Turing was voted the greatest person of the twentieth century by an audience poll conducted by the British Broadcasting Corporation in 2019, beating Pablo Picasso, Nelson Mandela and Dr Martin Luther King Jr, which is quite an achievement for someone who had to be kept largely out of the public eye during his lifetime for reasons of national security and who died when he was only 41 after being found guilty of homosexual acts, at a time when they were still criminal. But Alan Turing was no ordinary individual. If we don't hear much about the Turing machines he invented it's because today their successors are called computers. Alan Turing was a mathematical genius best remembered these days for his work at Bletchley Park, the top secret UK communications' centre during the Second World War, where Turing and others cracked and then deciphered German radio signals sent in a code its creators believed was unbreakable. Turing invented a machine that made this task possible and in so doing made a colossal* advance in the development of the information technology we use today.

---

* Nice choice of adjective – Turing's Bletchley Park machine was, of course, called Colossus.

17

Never Had It So Good

LISTEN WITH MOTHER

Listen with Mother was a 15-minute radio programme aired by the British Broadcasting Corporation between 16 January 1950 and 10 September, 32 years later. The target audience was young children and their mothers and the show was available every weekday at 1.45 in the afternoon, when little ones were digesting their lunch and their mothers were getting ready to listen to *Woman's Hour* – which, bizarrely, was first presented by a man on the grounds that he was a specialist 'in writing for and talking to women'! Over one million tuned in to *Listen with Mother* at its peak, but the growing appeal of television steadily eroded that core base until a survey in the mid-seventies revealed that as many long-distance lorry drivers as pre-schoolers listened to *Listen with Mother* each day. At the centre of each edition of *Listen with Mother* was a story that was always prefaced by the soothing enquiry-cum-injunction 'Are you sitting comfortably? Then I'll begin.' This style of intimate contact directed at each individual child (and HGV operative) gave *Listen with Mother* its distinctive tone, along with the recitation of nursery rhymes and the chanting of simple songs.

The wheels on the bus go round and round...

BILL AND BEN

Bill and Ben were a pair of puppets who appeared on British children's television for over 20 years from the early 1950s. Like Vladimir and Estragon in *Waiting for Godot*, Bill and Ben passed their time in a series of discussions and occasional encounters in the same location (in their case behind a potting shed in suburbia) while waiting for the return of 'the man who worked in the garden'. Instead of being dressed as tramps like the duo in the play,* Bill and Ben had to make do with old earthenware containers, after which they were named the Flower Pot Men. The surreal undercurrents permeating the show extended to the third character, a plant growing between Bill and Ben called Little Weed – whose voice, incidentally, was provided by the actress Denise Bryer, the first wife of *Just A Minute*'s very own Nicholas Parsons. One can only speculate what fun the scriptwriters must have had when their brand of flower pot power later found itself running in concert with smoking joints and psychedelia. Although Bill and Ben were way ahead of the game with their unique language and vocabulary, known as Oddle Poddle. As Ben would say, it was 'Flobabdob!'

---

* Samuel Beckett's play has been deployed in an earlier portion of this book in order momentarily to confuse readers seeking to work out the link between a medieval cleric and an Irish playwright. Here, the staging of this simple children's entertainment is elevated and dramatically enriched by comparing it with the one in which the main characters find themselves in *Waiting for Godot*. The fact that they too wait perpetually for a character who never appears presents the author with a pleasing conceit that gets everyone else wondering where the discourse is going just in time for the next red herring: the link between the flower pot men and the culture of flower power. Readers might be interested to know that this last topic is discussed shortly in greater detail (see page 221).

CRICK AND WATSON

Bill and Ben, Ant and Dec, Tom and Jerry, Morecambe and Wise, Holmes and Watson, these are the great double acts of recent times. But Crick and Watson – who they? Well, Francis Crick and James Watson are the two scientific researchers credited with the discovery of the molecular structure of DNA – and where would present-day police dramas on television be without them? In 1962, Crick and Watson, and their colleague Maurice Watkins, were awarded the Nobel Prize in Physiology or Medicine for their work. However, a fourth contributor missed out on the accolade. She was a chemist named Rosalind Franklin, who was no longer alive when the others were honoured, although people suspected she may have been overlooked because she was a woman. Accusations of poor scientific ethics were bandied about, but history now records Crick and Watson as principal contributors following the ground-breaking publication of their article on the subject in *Nature* nine years before the Swedish Academy selected them. Incidentally, a friend's DNA results came back with the surprising news he was 35 per cent German, one quarter Irish, the same English, half that French and the rest Pug.* Then it turned out his dog had licked the sample.

---

* **R** Clever circumlocution employed here to avoid repetition of 'per cent', while still delivering accurate proportions.

TAKE IT FROM HERE

Take It From Here was a radio comedy show broadcast from three years after the end of the Second World War until 1960 and created by two young scriptwriters, Frank Muir and Denis Norden. The writing team also including one Herbert Mostyn who didn't exist at all and whose name was simply the middle names of the pair of principal authors. *Take It From Here* introduced the listening public to a new brand of entertainment that went on to inspire many others. The formula blended comic songs with humorous dialogues, parodies and sketches. One firm favourite that became a mainstay of *Take It From Here* was a weekly sketch about a family called The Glums, in which Pa Glum was played by the moustachioed trombone-playing entertainer, Jimmy Edwards – the man who was first asked to chair *Just A Minute*, but couldn't do it because the recordings were to take place on a Sunday, a day he liked to keep free so he could play polo.* This rumbustious pater-familias had a son, a clueless dimwit named Ronald, engaged to an ever-patient fiancée, played first by the delightful Joy Nichols and later by the enchanting June Whitfield. In one episode, she asks, 'Oh, Ron, is there anything on your mind, beloved?' to which her gormless betrothed, after a long pause, replies, 'No, Eth.'

* **D** This is definitely deviation, but interesting nonetheless. Yes, Nicholas Parsons was originally invited to be a panellist on *Just A Minute*. He only became chairman because Jimmy Edwards was unavailable for the role.

THE WIZARD OF THE DRIBBLE

'The wizard of the dribble' was the nickname given to a celebrated footballer – not Lionel Messi, as his surname might suggest, but Stanley Matthews, the first to win the top European award for individual performance and reckoned by many to be the foremost British exponent of the beautiful game from his generation. Among his many achievements, he was also the only player to be knighted while still making professional appearances on the pitch. But being a 'Sir' was a far cry from the young wizard's childhood when he spent hours dribbling a ball around chairs placed in the kitchen or in the yard behind his terraced home in Stoke-on-Trent. The 'wizard of the dribble' spent 19 years in total with Stoke City: two spells, divided by 14 seasons at Blackpool. As an international, he won 54 England caps and represented his country at two World Cup finals. Amazingly, he was still active at the top level when he had passed his two score years and ten.* On his seventieth birthday I had the privilege of hosting a dinner in his honour and he was a model of gentlemanly modesty. He wouldn't look at the screen showing highlights from his illustrious career. He said it embarrassed him. He also told me how he was paid £5 a week when he started out as a young soccer player – 'that's quite enough for kicking a ball around a field'.

TACKLED BY A CHAIR

---

* Nice wordplay at the end, drawing an appropriate pun from 'score'.

SUPERMAC

Supermac can refer to a fast-food chain in Ireland, the England footballer Malcolm Macdonald, a brand of rainwear, or Maurice Harold Macmillan, UK prime minister for six years from 1957, and later first Earl of Stockton. Given that the title for this section of our *History of Britain* was trumpeted by the latter, we'll go with him. Supermac was the nickname given to our man by a cartoonist called Vicky in the late fifties. He had intended the moniker to be an insult. But his sally backfired when a lot of people took it as a compliment to a national leader who seemed to be steering the country towards an era of well-being and prosperity. Under his government living standards rose, the working week was reduced and a number of social reforms were introduced including improvements to pensions and child welfare. Supermac also oversaw the steady granting of independence to former colonies. However, his grip on power and events appeared to slip following a series of scandals that rocked his administration, most notably the Profumo affair. His own wife Dorothy's romantic liaison with another MP, Robert Boothby, is something he managed to rise above with dignity, so let's follow his example. Supermac was fond of Victorian novels and during his premiership was often found of an afternoon curled up on the sofa at 10 Downing Street with a favourite Trollope.

THE FIRST MINI

For me, the first Minnie was undoubtedly the delectable Minnie Mouse, the cartoon character created by Walt Disney back in the roaring twenties as the companion to Mickey. Imagine her white gloves, her perky bow, that polka-dotted dress, and feel the magic. That said, I suspect the first Mini we have in mind here is the compact motor vehicle that hit the showrooms in 1959, eclipsing foreign competition like German bubble cars and the Italian Fiat 500, and revolutionised small car design thereafter. The timing could not have been better. Britain was on the cusp of a decade of growth, liberation and fun. Mini was good, whether it was transistor radios, rising hemlines or cheeky little runabouts. But the Mini would become more than just an inexpensive easy-to-park automobile. In the middle of the Swinging Sixties Mini entrants came first in four successive Monte Carlo rallies and the Mini achieved even greater international acclaim in the movie *The Italian Job* – in which the famous vehicular quartet drove through the sewers of Coventry masquerading as the drains of Turin. The arrival of the Mini also gave rise to the strange practice of trying to squeeze as many people inside one as possible. The record for the first Mini occupancy stands at 27! Even the larger modern Mini only added one more. Forty years after its arrival the Mini was voted second in the Global Car of the Century competition, one behind the Model T Ford.

THE ARCHERS

The Archers is a radio drama series that has been broadcast by the British Broadcasting Corporation since 1951. As the world's longest-running soap opera it was originally billed as 'an everyday story of country folk' set in and around the fictitious village of Ambridge, located in the equally fabricated county of Borsetshire, in the English Midlands. *The Archers* was originally conceived as a means of sharing information with agricultural producers to improve efficiency in the post-war era when people still endured rationing and food shortages. But *The Archers* soon found a much wider audience and within three years it shared jointly with *Take It From Here* (see page 207) the annual award for most entertaining programme. Unlike many shows of its type, *The Archers* has always responded adroitly to major events in the wider world. But its most controversial move in this direction was the dramatic death of a lead character (the young and recently married Grace Archer), which had the nation transfixed beside its radios on the very night that the Beeb's first television rival (Associated-Rediffusion) was launched. Incidentally, my Uncle Wilfrid's sister was married to a lovely actor called Arnold Peters who played Jack Woolley in *The Archers* for 21 years. Oh yes, I've known 'em all.

WHO WAS DIANA DORS?

'Who was Diana Dors?' may have seemed a ridiculous question in the 1950s and early sixties when the blonde bombshell, Britain's answer to Jayne Mansfield and Marilyn Monroe, was widely photographed and watched in cinemas. But 'Who was Diana Dors?' was a valid enquiry to those who knew her and for the lady herself. When she was born in Swindon in the year one thousand nine hundred and thirty-one, her mother didn't know whether the baby's father was her husband or the man she'd been having an affair with. Diana Dors came into being when the young actress had to sign the contract for her screen debut. Until that point, Diana Dors had been called Diana Fluck (after her 'paternal' family) but, as she later explained, the producers asked her to adopt a different one, 'I suppose they were afraid that if my real name was in lights and one of them blew …'! Dors, the maiden appellation of her maternal grandmother, avoided that potential calamity and the embarrassing headlines that would certainly have followed.* (For the sake of clarity, the mistaken surname that gave rise to this concern was not Fluke.)

* This book is for a family audience, otherwise I'd tell you the story of the nervous vicar who, welcoming Diana back to open the church fete near her childhood home, said, 'The world knows her as Diana Dors. Here we think of her always as Diana Clunt.'

THE ROUTEMASTER BUS

I couldn't get my fridge to work this morning, so I took the bus instead. Boom-tish! I didn't like being a bus driver. I was convinced people were talking behind my back. Whey-hey! Routemaster buses, London's double-deckers, are as much a symbol of Britain as the Union Jack, the Houses of Parliament and Brexit. In 2006 Routemaster buses formed part of the list of Britain's top-ten design icons along with the Mini (see page 210), the capital's tube map, the World Wide Web and the red telephone box. The first four Routemaster buses were introduced into service in the early fifties and remained a key part of our public transport network for the next half century. They became such a part of national daily life that an entire TV sitcom, *On the Buses*, and its film spin-offs were centred on them. Routemaster buses were designed with distinctive open rear platforms, which made it easy for passengers to get on and off, but also made them very chilly in winter, to the point where travellers would enquire, 'What is the difference between a bus driver and a cold?' to be told, 'One knows the stops, the other stops* the nose.'

---

* **R** Bold play, teasing other contestants first with a repetition of 'driver' and then with the blatant repetition of 'stops'. It would have been safer, of course, to have substituted the second usage of 'stops' with a different verb: 'blocks', 'obstructs', 'plugs' for example. But the pun always wins over pragmatism, trusting on the winning whistle following just two words later.

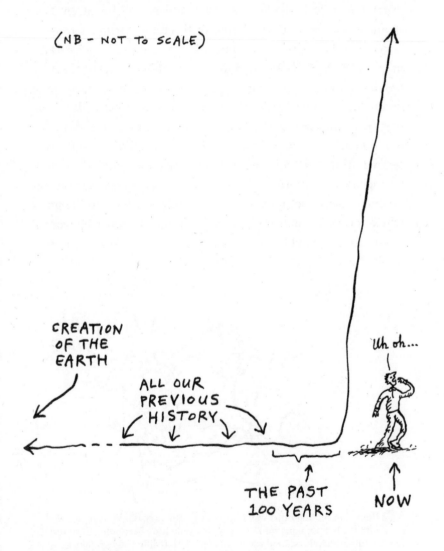

18

The Swinging Sixties

JOHN, PAUL, GEORGE AND RINGO

We know who they are. Spare a thought for Pete, their original drummer, who fell by the wayside early on and therefore isn't one of this illustrious near-immortal quartet. Yes, John (Lennon), Paul (McCartney), George (Harrison) and Ringo (Starr) were a Liverpudlian quartet who took the pop music world by storm six decades ago as the Beatles. Nicknamed the Fab Four, they have come to be regarded as the most influential rock band in history and one of the main drivers of the iconic culture of the Swinging Sixties. Their songs had widespread appeal from the horsey community, whose favourite was 'Hay Chewed', to the fans of fresh fruit whose only regret was that they didn't colour the submarine in their well-known maritime song green rather than yellow: that would have made it sublime. Like a lot of people who listened avidly to them, I'm addicted to collecting their LPs and I don't mind admitting that I need 'Help!' Influential as John, Paul, George and Ringo were there was one genre of popular vocal entertainment that they did not have any influence over. That was hip hop, but they couldn't claim to do everything – they weren't grasshoppers after all.

I'm Pete. — From the Beatles.

TWIGGY

Twiggy was the professional name of the present-day Dame Lesley Lawson, who was the iconic British fashion model of the second half of the 1960s. In her mid-teens, Twiggy skyrocketed to international fame as the personification of what the *New York Times* called 'a new kind of streamlined, androgynous sex appeal'. She was named the face of the year immediately after the mid-point of the decade and voted British Woman of the Year in the same 12-month period.* But this took her completely by surprise. 'At sixteen, I was a funny, skinny little thing, all eyelashes and legs' she later admitted. 'And then, suddenly people told me it was gorgeous. I thought they had gone mad.' The Twiggy look comprised three seminal features: a stick-thin figure, a haircut that was boyishly short and distinctive dark *cils* (as the French call them) that required three layers of false cilia to achieve the desired effect. After switching her career focus to acting and singing, Twiggy was rewarded with two Golden Globe awards for *The Boyfriend* and a Tony nomination for her Broadway debut in the musical *My One and Only*.

---

* **R** Readers may have guessed, if they didn't already know, that the year referred to is 1966. This obviously presents serious challenges if the repetition of 'six' is to be avoided. The tactics resorted to may appear clumsy and contrived, but by the standards of playing *Just A Minute* they amount to a tour de force.

THE TRIAL OF LADY CHATTERLEY'S LOVER

The trial of *Lady Chatterley's Lover* took place following the British publication of that unexpurgated novel by Penguin Books in 1960. David Herbert Lawrence, bearded playwright and randy novelist, had written the book over 30 years earlier, but *Lady Chatterley's Lover* had been widely banned on the grounds of obscenity and moral corruption. When prosecutors lost the action, it was hailed as a landmark in the freedom of speech and the breaking down of outdated taboos – and three million copies flew off the shelves. But not everyone appeared to understand what the fuss was about. The graphic account of the affair between Constance Chatterley and her husband's employee in charge of field sports was reviewed in the US outdoor magazine *Field & Stream** which commended the 'many passages on pheasant raising, the apprehending of poachers, ways to control vermin, and the chores and duties of the professional gamekeeper. Unfortunately,' it continued, 'one is obliged to wade through pages of extraneous material in order to discover and savor these sidelights on the management of a Midlands sporting estate, and in this reviewer's opinion this book cannot take the place of J. R. Miller's *Practical Gamekeeping*.'

---

* **D** This account of the celebrated review might well invite a challenge for deviation. However, a clever twist to the subject might allow the player to dodge it and retain the right to keep speaking. The subject title reads 'The trial of Lady Chatterley's Lover' and the reader naturally focuses initially on the historic legal proceedings brought against Penguin Books under the Obscene Publications Act 1959. However, the subject does not implicitly restrict us to the legal proceedings against Penguin Books under the Obscene Publications Act 1959 and their aftermath. The passage quoted from the *Field & Stream* review focuses on the duties of the gamekeeper in the story, some of which may be regarded as burdensome and might thus be rightly described as a trial. Given that Mellors, the gamekeeper in question, was also conducting an illicit and physically demanding affair as his employer's wife's lover, that too could legitimately constitute a trial at times. On both counts, then, quoting from the review might, far from deviating from the subject, rather develop and expand the topic to give a fuller exposition.

PETER COOK AND DUDLEY MOORE

Peter Cook and Dudley Moore formed a double act in the 1960s which redefined comedy on stage and on the screen. Peter Cook, tall and debonair, Dudley Moore short and sprightly, regarded their relationship as 'a marriage of opposites', which gelled when they formed half of the smash-hit revue *Beyond the Fringe* (the other pair being Alan Bennett and Jonathan Miller). That show brought the humour of student burlesques to wider public attention on both sides of the Atlantic. Peter Cook had been writing scripts for leading comedians like Kenneth Williams since his undergraduate days at Cambridge; Dudley Moore, an Oxford organ scholar, had his own jazz trio. Television programmes like *Not Only … But Also*, *Pete and Dud* and *Goodbye Again* gave full rein to their talents interweaving sketches with musical interludes and comic songs. Regular favourites included the 'Dagenham Dialogues', rambling surreal conversations, often conducted over a pint in a pub. Their success transferred to the cinema in the films *The Wrong Box*, *Bedazzled* and *Monte Carlo or Bust*, before Dudley Moore settled in Hollywood to pursue an independent movie career, where at a height of 1 metre 59, he was known as the original sex thimble.

Fluck ⟶ CLIVE   Clunt

CLIVE   DEREK

THE PROFUMO AFFAIR

The Profumo affair was a political scandal in the 1960s which captivated British public attention, rocked the establishment and heralded the end of 13 years of Conservative government. At its centre was John Profumo, Secretary of State for War. Other figures in the notorious turn of events were: Lord Astor, whose mother Nancy was the first woman seated as a MP; Captain Yevgeny Ivanov, a naval attaché at the Soviet embassy; Stephen Ward, the go-between for the other principals; and two young women struggling to launch their careers as models – Mandy Rice-Davies and Christine Keeler. The latter had a brief affair with Jack Profumo, while also conducting a similarly intimate relationship with the Russian diplomat. As the Cold War heated, rumours circulated about a possible espionage triangle, forcing Profumo to tell parliament that he was innocent of any misconduct. When this was proved to be a lie, he resigned, his intermediary killed himself, the girl at the centre of the affair served six months in prison for perjury, and Prime Minister Harold Macmillan left office on the grounds of ill health. Such can be the consequences of illicit rumpy-pumpy.

FLOWER POWER

Flower Power was an anti-Vietnam War slogan that developed into a movement in the late 1960s. It originated in the writing of American beat poet Allen Ginsberg as a way of turning protests against the military conflict in Southeast Asia into spectacles that affirmed universal love. Demonstrators who supported Flower Power were encouraged to hand out flowers to law enforcement officers, politicians and members of the public as a way of defusing hostility towards their demand for peace and an end to the fighting. But Flower Power quickly migrated from its Californian roots in a wave of rallies, marches, music and festivities characterised by the Summer of Love in the seventh years of the aforementioned decade. Flower Power had a cultural legacy that extended far beyond its pacifist exhortations into the work of iconic bands like Jefferson Airplane and the Grateful Dead, while Scott McKenzie's song 'San Francisco (Be Sure to Wear Flowers in Your Hair)' became its unofficial anthem. And the influence of Flower Power endures long after its young protagonists aged and matured. People ask why former hippies make good accountants, but the answer is simple: they're from a counter-culture.

1... 2... 3...

NOTTING HILL CARNIVAL

The Notting Hill Carnival has been a feature of London life since the first was held in 1966. Spread over the annual August Bank Holiday weekend it is a celebration of Caribbean lifestyles and entertainments that takes place on the streets of the eponymous area of Kensington. In its early days the Notting Hill Carnival mirrored many of the social changes that were taking place in Britain at that time, notably an evolving adjustment in race relations and the growing importance of popular culture in shaping the way people lived, enjoyed themselves and viewed the world at large. Music has always been a key component of the Notting Hill Carnival. In its fourth year two bands provided the auditory entertainment, though by the time of the Golden Jubilee 42 hours of live video coverage were provided by the likes of Channel One, (that *Just A Minute* favourite) Deviation, Gladdy Wax, King Tubbys, Nasty Love and Saxon Sound. Vigorous dancing, decorated floats, exotic outfits and the heady aromas of street food continue to make the Notting Hall Carnival a landmark event to round off summer in the capital.

(I CAN'T GET NO) SATISFACTION

'(I Can't Get No) Satisfaction', often abbreviated to 'Satisfaction', was a song released by rock band the Rolling Stones in the summer of 1965. It brought the group its initial chart-topping hit in the USA and was among the world's most popular musical numbers, being voted thirty-first in the top 500 all-time greatest. Written by Keith Richards and Mick Jagger, '(I Can't Get No) Satisfaction' addressed two sources of satisfaction (or the lack of it): disillusionment with the commercialisation of contemporary life and the lack of carnal satisfaction in an era of increasingly free love. On both counts it was regarded as subversive and for a while was only available to British audiences through the broadcasts of pirate radio stations. Paradoxically, the title means the opposite to what is implied. 'I can't get no satisfaction' is a double negative, which effectively means 'I can get satisfaction'.* But syntax and grammatical accuracy may not have been at the forefront of their minds when its creators composed the famous lyrics which brought them the acclaim and success in America that they always wanted.

---

* One can only admire and applaud those who are able to undertake this kind of close textual analysis while simultaneously focusing on getting to the end of their minute-long delivery without being challenged for one of the trio of tombstone tripwires.

THE 1966 WORLD CUP

I remember it well. The 1966 World Cup featured a series of memorable firsts and lasts. On 30 July of that year England (the host nation) beat West Germany 4–2 to become world champions, which hasn't happened subsequently. The 1966 World Cup also saw the introduction of competition mascots: our inaugural one being somewhat dubiously called Willie. The 1966 World Cup was also the occasion when its Jules Rimet trophy was stolen by an as yet unidentified thief who, realising the complications of trying to flog a world-famous lump of solid gold worth £30,000, wrapped it in newspaper and shoved it under a car in south London where it was discovered by a dog named Pickles. He became the first canine to be invited to a World Cup-winning dinner, was named the man's best friend of the year and received a 12-month supply of food courtesy of pet-feed manufacturers Spillers. And the 'concluding events'? The 1966 World Cup was the final one to be broadcast on television in black and white, and Geoff Hurst's ultimate goal brought him a unique World Cup hat-trick. In 2021, I am proud to say, I had the honour of presenting Sir Geoffrey with an Oldie of the Year accolade as he turned 80.

THE WORLD CUP and SAUCER

HAROLD WILSON'S PIPE

Harold Wilson's pipe was as much a symbol of his time as British prime minister as Winston Churchill's cigar (see page 192) was of his. Voted the British Pipesmokers' Council pipe user of the year in 1965, Harold Wilson deployed his pipe to serve a number of purposes. It was the ideal prop to help him craft the everyday fatherly image that the public warmed to. His pipe also provided a useful distraction when he needed time to gather his thoughts. However, as a senior aide confided a dozen years after Harold Wilson had died in the mid-nineties, the pipe was largely for public show. He was seldom seen with it in private (he actually preferred to smoke cigars) and, even when he did have it on display, the pipe wasn't always lit because he would soon have to put it away in a pocket. When a statue commemorating him was commissioned, his widow Mary insisted that it should not have a pipe for fear it would be seen as a caricature; that would have sent Harold Wilson's legacy ashtray.

SIR KEN DODD

Sir Ken Dodd is a national treasure we have already encountered in this book (see page 170); he had some wise things to say about the invention of cat's eyes. And the range of his powers extended far beyond road safety. Ken Dodd was destined to be an entertainer. 'My dad always knew I was going to be a comedian,' he used to tell audiences. 'When I was a baby he said, "Is this a joke?"' But Ken Dodd had to learn his craft the hard way. As he explained when discussing psychoanalysis, 'The trouble with Freud is that he never played the Glasgow Empire on a Saturday night after Rangers and Celtic had both lost.' A trouper to the end, he understood human frailty, especially his own, observing in later life, 'I always feel at home in theatres like this, because we're about the same age.' But in his prime, Ken Dodd was unbeatable, making it into the record books for delivering 1500 jokes in three and a half hours. What would the Diddy Men have to say about that? You tell me.

DODDY → Yarroo! ← DIDDY MEN

SIR CLIFF RICHARD OBE

Sir Cliff Richard is among the top-selling music artists ever with worldwide record sells exceeding 250 million. He is credited with Britain's first authentic rock and roll record: 'Move It' released in 1958, which many believe laid the foundations for the success of future stars like the Beatles and the Rolling Stones. At the beginning of his career, Cliff Richard was styled as a hell-raising singer and this country's answer to Elvis Presley. Until the arrival of the Mersey sound in the sixties Cliff Richard and his backing performers the Shadows were the foremost home-grown pop group. As a solo artiste, Cliff Richard found new fans with more middle-of-the road numbers, such as 'Congratulations', the British Eurovision Song contest entry in 1968 which lost to the entry from Spain, catchily entitled 'La La La',[*] by a single point – possibly because the vote had been rigged by Spanish dictator Francisco Franco.[†] His works continued into maturity and beyond following a principle that has guided him throughout, 'Those of us who have something to offer have to be prepared to give all the time.'

[*] **R** Oh no, he should have seen that coming. 'La repeated twice more' has to be the song title in the world of *Just A Minute*

[†] **D** A well worked nugget of contemporary history dropped in towards the end of the minute-long discourse throws off the reader and eats up time, while staying close enough to the subject to fend off challenges for deviation.

WHERE WE LIVE

I live in
the past.

I live in
the present.

I live in
the future.

19

TV and Radio

JUST A MINUTE

Over the years I have appeared in scores of panel games on radio and TV, and even devised a few, but *Just A Minute* stands way above the crowd. The trouble with most other shows is that they record two hours and more and then edit it down to 28 minutes, so no one needs to be on their mettle throughout. *Just A Minute* is much more exciting, recorded in real time and against the clock. When you listen, you don't get edited highlights: you hear what happened. I have been taking part in *Just A Minute* since 1982 and the only rule I have is not to try to tell jokes: invariably you trip up as you get towards the punchline. The late Clement Freud holds the record as the game's most frequent winner, followed by Paul Merton and Derek Nimmo. (I come in at No. 7, just ahead of Sheila Hancock, just behind Tony Hawks.) Freud was the master of coming up with a challenge with just three seconds to go and utterly ruthless as a player. If you sat next to him, he'd find all sorts of ways of distracting you if he sensed you were about to make a challenge. Once, deliberately, he spilled a glass of water onto me just as I was hitting my stride. In the early years, Kenneth Williams was the undoubted star of the show. He still holds the record as the player to have achieved the largest number of uninterrupted minutes, ahead of Freud and Derek Nimmo. (I am at No 7 again, sandwiched between Sue Perkins and Sheila Hancock). The programme suited Kenneth's peculiar gifts perfectly: he could mix his amazing erudition (all self-taught) with a range of extraordinary comic voices and a natural genius as a raconteur. Towards the end of his life, he told me that *Just A Minute* was about the only thing he still really enjoyed. Some assumed that when Williams died the programme would die with him. Not so. A whole new generation of funny folk are now playing the game and it is being produced by bright young things who weren't even alive when the programme was first broadcast in 1967.*

---

* **R** This is way, way, way longer than just a minute! And it's full of repetitions. Yes and yes, but isn't it interesting? Occasionally, when someone is on a roll, we allow them to keep going beyond the normally allowed 60 seconds.

NICHOLAS PARSONS

Ah, Nicholas Parsons. We think of him now as the smooth-talking silver-tongued chairman of the world's longest-running radio panel show, *Just A Minute*. But – as he would very much want me to remind you – there was so much more to him than that. He had half-a-dozen careers and he revelled in all of them. As an actor, he appeared in several of the films made in the 1950s and '60s by the celebrated Boulting Brothers, as well as in a couple of *Carry Ons*. He starred in the West End in *Boeing-Boeing*.* He was a knock-out in stockings and suspenders in *The Rocky Horror Show*. Right up until the year before he died, in two thousand and twenty aged 96, he was touring the country in his one-man show celebrating the life and nonsense verse of Edward Lear. As a comedian, he performed at the famous Windmill Theatre after the Second World War and he was still doing stand-up at the Edinburgh Fringe when he was five years shy of becoming a centenarian. On the box, he was the straight man to the comic Arthur Haynes and hosted the ITV quiz, *Sale of the Century* – once upon a time the most-watched programme in the land with an audience of twenty million plus. He also presented a pioneering chat show on the wireless, *Look Who's Talking*; he wrote several books; he collected antique clocks. He never stopped until the final whistle went.

---

* **R** Repetition! But you could argue that it should be allowed – like yoyo. You'd be wrong.

DOCTOR WHO

Doctor Who is a science-fiction television programme that has been aired by the British Broadcasting Corporation for almost six decades. The central character is a Time Lord, centuries old, who has a number of useful life skills. The Doctor can move forwards and backwards in chronology. The Doctor's physical age is equally flexible. And, most accomplished of all, the Doctor appears to be able to live for eternity in perfect harmony with a selection of companions while cooped up inside an old-fashioned police box. *Doctor Who* was first transmitted on Saturday 23 November 1963, the day after the assassination of US President John F. Kennedy. As one might expect, referring to the main member of the cast as Doctor Who is no accident. To date the Doctor has gone through 13 human manifestations, the most recent of which bears a striking resemblance to the actor Jodie Whittaker. My favourite was the be-scarfed Tom Baker and I had a soft spot, too, for Jon Pertwee. Although it's rated as the longest-running and most successful TV show of its kind, *Doctor Who* has not been without critics. Some complain that the Doctor is a dreadful procrastinator, because s/he leaves everything for earlier.

Just A Minute?

No problem.

I simply stop time, have a think, start it again...

...and win every time.

DAD'S ARMY

Dad's Army is a situation comedy about a seaside platoon of the Home Guard during the Second World War. First shown in 1968, it is still being screened in countries around the world more than half a century later. A trial screening to selected viewers was not well received and the producers wisely kept this buried for several weeks until the initial transmissions quickly developed an enthusiastic fan base. Nine series were recorded, with a total of four score episodes, followed by a couple of feature films, a stage version and one for radio. *Dad's Army* opened with the song 'Who Do You Think You Are Kidding, Mr Hitler?', which sounded just like a contemporary number from the first half of the forties. It was actually a gentle pastiche with lyrics written by one of the creators, Jimmy Perry, but having it sung by period favourite Bud Flanagan made it sound totally authentic. Ironically, the Local Defence Volunteers (the term initially used for members of Dad's Army and their fellows) were largely forgotten when *Dad's Army* hit the screens in one thousand nine hundred and sixty-eight.* Today it is one of the better remembered Allied armed detachments from those years of conflict.

---

* **R** A familiar tactic, but one still worth noting especially as it has been deployed so close to the end of the author's minute, is rendering dates in this manner (inspired by speakers of the French language, no doubt) to avoid repetition of words like 'nineteen'.

DESERT ISLAND DISCS

Desert Island Discs is a long-running radio series broadcast by the Beeb and when I say it is of lengthy longevity, I'm not kidding: it was first aired in late January 1942. Each week a guest is invited to select eight 'discs' (usually music, but see below), a book and a luxury item that they would need if they were to be cast away on a desert island. I featured 69 years after the first transmission and found it an honour and a nightmare. Some time before I had met the great Roy Plomley, who devised *Desert Island Discs* and presented it for its first four decades. So I was looking forward to chatting through the outline of the programme over a relaxing lunch (the creator used to entertain his castaways at his club). But with the charming Kirsty Young as my crisp interrogator in 2011, I had to make do with a cup of coffee at 8.55am and then we were off – though not as I had expected. It had taken weeks to select my discs, my wife having dismissed my first set (of largely spoken material, since that means so much more to me than music) as 'Pretentious, attention-seeking, ridiculous.' Now the presenter and her producer had rearranged my order – because they liked 'to mix it up a bit'! And so they did. They'd got the wrong recording of Laurence Olivier's Othello (the correct one was later substituted). I was reduced to tears hearing again the voice of a dear and much missed friend. And then I managed to speak about my entire life for an hour without once mentioning my spouse. Luckily, this was spotted before I left and we slipped in a bit extra to plug the gap. Now I come to think of it, *Desert Island Discs*, on which I was symbolically marooned and alone, probably saved my marriage.*

---

* Occasionally one lets a player on a roll continue beyond the minute mark and so it is in this very personal account of what must surely have been a memorable contribution to the legacy of the BBC.

CORONATION STREET

Coronation Street is the name given to 87 thoroughfares in the UK along with 171 Coronation Roads, 93 Coronation Avenues, 2 Coronation Mews and 8 Coronation Squares. The one that is sometimes mistaken as a Coronation Street for its television coverage at royal ceremonials is the Mall in London, which runs up to the front door of Buckingham Palace. Probably the best-known Coronation Street is not a real street at all. This is the Coronation Street which forms the central location in the ITV soap opera *Coronation Street*, that has been seminal viewing for 'Corrie' fans since it was first broadcast way back in 1960. This cobbled street, in the equally fictitious northern town of Weatherfield, features a number of exteriors that regularly appear in the show. These include a row of terraced dwellings, a few townhouses, The Kabin (a newsagent's), D&S Alahan's (a grocery shop), a factory and the Rovers Return. The latter is not a reception centre for stray pets, but a public house where members of the cast frequently congregate to chew the fat and advance the storyline for the benefit of the six million viewers that tune in to each episode.

Rover. You returned.

BLUE PETER

'Blue Peter' is the name given to the maritime signal flag featuring a blue background with a white rectangle at its centre. It is flown to indicate that a ship is ready to sail, although in the canon of nautical communication Blue Peter also represents the number 2 and, as might be expected, the letter P. It was this pennant that inspired the long-running TV show *Blue Peter*, which has been transmitted by the British Broadcasting Corporation since October 1958. The story goes that the Blue Peter was displayed on a ferry plying the River Mersey, which was used as the setting for *Children's Television Club*, an entertainment pitched at youngsters aged between five and those three years senior.[*] This opened with the presenter, Judith Chalmers, standing at the bottom of the gangplank welcoming viewers aboard. The old name was swiftly dumped in favour of *Blue Peter*, which promised 'a voyage of adventure' in every programme. That applied to the presenters too. Although constructing things out of recycled domestic produce, attending to an assortment of pets and participating in hair-raising escapades did launch many successful TV[†] careers.

who thought up this stupid stunt?!

JOHN NOAKES

Help!

---

[*] **R** Clever avoidance of the repetition of 'eight'.
[†] **R** Repetition of TV, Gyles!

SUE PERKINS ON ...
BLUE PETER

Blue Peter was created by John Hunter Blair in 1958 as a way of stealth-promoting the wide-ranging uses of sticky-backed plastic. It created generations of exhausted parents and children who would sit, late into the night, making scale models of Tracy Island out of washing-up liquid bottles and sponge scourers. The golden era of *Blue Peter* came after a decade or so with the Fab Four: Valerie Singleton, John Noakes, Lesley Judd and Peter Purves. Their tenure coincided with an almost breathtaking disregard by British television broadcasters for the health and safety of their workforce. As a result, presenters would routinely perform adrenal-ised stunts without training or personal protection; walking a barely tethered lion into a newsagent, climbing Nelson's Column minus a harness, concertina-ing a spine on the Cresta Run or sliding in an elephant's poop as it charged round the studio. Pete tended not to participate in the physical stuff, choosing instead to make an Advent Candle from clothes hangers while dressed as a Regency dandy. Pets were a key part of *Blue Peter*'s success, with Shep the sheepdog living for over 30 years. Freda the tortoise also enjoyed a long innings, though later sued her employers for Tippex-poisoning after having had her name painted on her back at each and every hibernation.

ONLY FOOLS AND HORSES

'Only fools and horses' are the first four words of the time-honoured cockney turn of phrase 'Only fools and horses work', implying that anyone with something between their ears will find a way of making a living without having to put in serious effort. This premise and statement form the theme and title to the enormously successful sitcom *Only Fools and Horses*, which was aired through the 1980s until the first year of the following decade. The plot lines in *Only Fools and Horses* centred on the efforts of Derek 'Del Boy' and his young brother Rodney to make millions through a variety of dodgy scams and schemes undertaken by way of their family 'business', Trotters Independent Traders, most of which were conducted on the black market. *Only Fools and Horses* became one of the most popular comedy shows ever to appear on British television. One Christmas special in the mid-nineties attracted a lovely-jubbly, record audience of 24.3 million viewers – and statistics never lie, as the elder character said to his sibling, 'everything between you and I is split straight down the middle: 60-40.'

FLEABAG

Fleabag is a British television phenomenon, a TV tragicomedy that started on stage, migrated to the edgy third viewing channel of the Beeb before (deep breath) making it on to the mainstream. The writer, inspiration and lead in *Fleabag* is Phoebe Waller-Bridge. (Attentive readers of this book may remember her from an earlier entry about 'The Best Bond'; see page 188). *Fleabag* started its rise to fame as a one-woman play at the 2013 Edinburgh Festival Fringe where it picked up an award. The television premier followed three years later and the second series concluded 21 months after that. *Fleabag* won numerous accolades for its writing, acting and the unique portrayal of its central character. *Fleabag* is unconventional in many respects. Fleabag herself regularly breaks the fourth wall to communicate directly with her audience and all the filthiest vocabulary in one episode is sung in Latin. Such has been its impact that 'fleabagging' is now well established on social media as a term for the destructive practice of dating the wrong people time and again, even when the relationship is manifestly doomed from the outset.

PLANET EARTH

Planet Earth is a television wonder produced by the British Broadcasting Corporation's Natural History Unit and first screened in 2006. It was narrated by David Attenborough who bookended *Planet Earth* with these remarks at the beginning:

> *A hundred years ago, there were one and a half billion people on Earth. Now, over [four times that number] crowd our fragile planet. But even so, there are still places barely touched by humanity. This series will take you to the last wildernesses and show you the planet and its wildlife as you have never seen them before.*

and these at the end:

> *Our planet is still full of wonders. As we explore them, so we gain not only understanding, but power. It's not just the future of the whale that today lies in our hands: it's the survival of the natural world in all parts of the living planet. We can now destroy or we can cherish. The choice is ours.* *

Between them lay 11 hour-long episodes that had taken five years to make and commanded the largest budget the Beeb ever committed to a documentary of this type. But it paid off handsomely, winning widespread international acclaim and a slew of major awards.

---

* Why struggle to come up with one's own words when others can speak for you? Here's a classic example of the well-judged quotation that brings eloquence, authority and accuracy on to the given subject purely through the recitation of what someone else said on the subject.

SIR DAVID ATTENBOROUGH

Sir David Attenborough is a master of British broadcasting on both sides of the camera – and the microphone. After what one might politely call a soft opening for the Beeb's second television channel, David Attenborough became its controller, gingered up the network and reshaped it into the distinctive outlet it became for the following decades. Under his leadership ground-breaking shows were commissioned, among them: *Monty Python's Flying Circus*, *Chronicle*, *Call My Bluff*, *Civilisation*, *The Ascent of Man* and *The Old Grey Whistle Test*. Sports fans got a boost with the introduction of *Match of the Day* and *Pot Black* (where the snooker balls of different hues made a virtue of newly introduced colour TV). In addition to these administrative triumphs, David Attenborough never lost his enthusiasm for presenting natural history programmes and with *Life on Earth*, which first aired in 1979, he began a succession of outstanding wildlife film documentaries that raised that medium to a new level of technical skill and audience appreciation which continues to this day. In association with this body of work, David Attenborough has become a respected authority on the dual challenges of climate change and environmental degradation, for which he has been admired worldwide.

Unfortunately, despite all his work... I'm doomed.

MR BEAN

Mr Bean is the hapless central character in the sitcom *Mr Bean*, who has been described by one of his creators as 'a child in a grown man's body'. Mr Bean is portrayed in the series by the actor, comedian and writer Rowan Sebastian Atkinson (whose full name is given here in order to reveal that it's an anagram of 'I, an artist, so known as Bean' – which has to be worth the detour, you must admit).* Mr Bean should feature in any British Hall of Fame since in a number of respects he personifies elements of the national personality that have cropped up during this survey of our national history. Let's start with his appearance. In his brown tweed jacket, white shirt, thin red tie, dung-coloured trousers and black shoes he is more Bean Brummel than Beau, like most British men down the centuries. Self-absorbed and highly competitive (ring any bells?), he gets himself into the kind of scrapes most people would sensibly avoid – a metaphor for Brexit perhaps? However, Mr Bean somehow manages to contrive unique and usually absurd solutions to his dilemmas and here one is spoilt for choice with earlier parallels: our first prime minister who kept the job for 20 years springs to mind, as do early attempts to invent television, the evacuation from Dunkirk, or the Millennium Dome. Yes, Mr Bean could have been responsible for all of these – and plenty more!†

---

* **D** Bold play here, acknowledging a small detour from the topic and tempting a challenge for deviation, when in fact the author has stayed within ten words of the subject title.

† **R** 'Cut out all these exclamation points. An exclamation point is like laughing at your own joke.' – F. Scott Fitzgerald … Isn't this where we came in? Repetition! Oops, sorry. Repetition.

PEPPA PIG

Good old Peppa – she is the salt of the earth. Her tail is very interesting. This funny little character, first seen in 2004, is anthropomorphic, not an easy word for her target audience to master – for Peppa Pig strikes a chord with anyone who has the mind of a three-year-old. I know that the Head of Channel 4 Comedy is a particular fan. Even the Royal Shakespeare Company's finest production of *A Midsummer Night's Dream* didn't have a finer Snout. Her trotters certainly eclipse those in *Only Fools and Horses*. Not until I listened to Aaron Copland's 'I Bought Me a Cat' did I discover that pigs like Peppa are supposed to make the noise 'Griffey, Griffey'.* Clearly my knowledge of our porcine friends is woefully inadequate if I wish to sustain a career in the entertainment industry. Without a doubt, potty, pink Peppa Pig is an institution. Some would even say she belongs in one.

---

* **R** Repetition of 'Griffey'.

TIMELINE SHOWING THE HISTORY
WE LEARNT AT SCHOOL

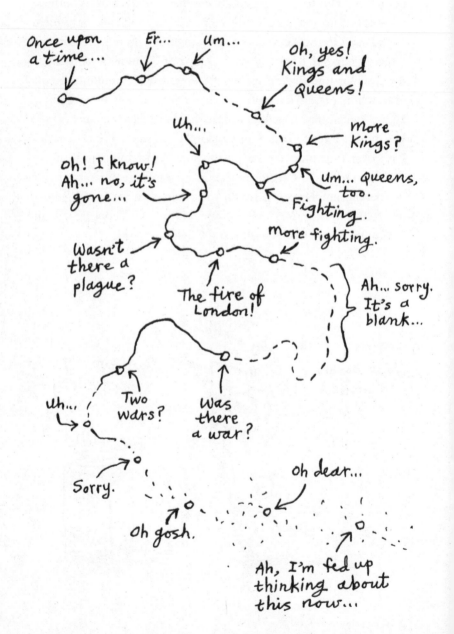

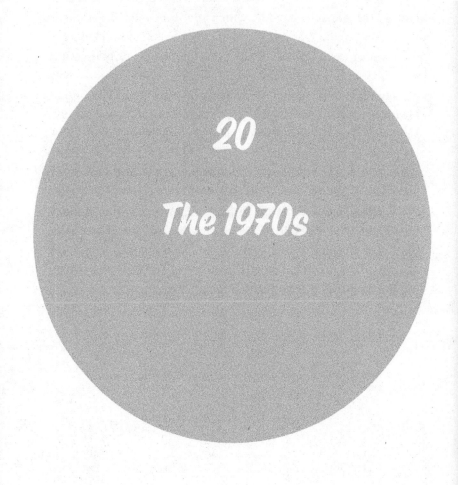

20

The 1970s

GEORGE BEST

George Best was a football player who in many respects personified the 1970s. Best had enjoyed a meteoric career in the second
half of the previous decade, which saw him named European
Footballer* of the Year and voted sixth in the poll to find Player of
the Century. As a brilliant winger and formidable dribbler of the
ball, George Best combined pace, skill, balance and control with
the agility to jink around defenders and unerringly score goals.
He helped Manchester United to notable league titles and the epic
European Cup victory ten years after the club had suffered devastating losses in the Munich air crash. Off the field, George Best's
dark good looks and pop-star following made him one of the
best-known young men of his day, with a succession of glamorous girlfriends and a lifestyle to match. However, a long-running
battle with the bottle and declining prowess saw his fortunes wane
and after revelling in the high life of the Swinging Sixties, the
years that followed were ones of controversy and decline, confirming that George's best was behind him.

---

* **R** It's a moot point whether 'Footballer' is a repetition of the earlier
'football'. It could be argued that a 'footballer' could not so describe himself, or
herself, without recourse to a football. However, that argument breaks down
when the term 'football' is seen in an international perspective. In Australia, for
instance, rugby (union and league) is frequently referred to as both 'football'
and 'footie'. In the USA, 'football' is immediately taken to mean the American
version of the game; association football being classified as 'soccer'.

SAYING GOODBYE TO POUNDS, SHILLINGS AND PENCE

Saying goodbye to pounds, shillings and pence came about on 15 February 1971. The day before, the feast of St Valentine, British people had been using cash as their forebears had for centuries past, when a pound comprised 20 shillings, with each of those consisting of 12 pence, making 240 pennies to the pound. This use dated back to ancient times when Roman money was divided into the librum, solidus and denarius, hence the £sd by which our coinage was known until Decimal Day. From then onwards, the pound was split into 100 pence and we said goodbye forever to the denominations we had known and loved. The shilling (or bob), the half-crown and the threepenny bit all disappeared. Public demand retained the sixpence (or tanner), but that too had gone within a decade. There were folk who weren't happy with the new money, but they were the kind who dislike all change. Others refused to believe that working with decimals was easier than calculating cash as they were used to. But they were simply missing the point. For what it's worth, I never believed in decimalisation. If God had wanted us to go decimal, he would not have given Our Lord a dozen disciples.

ZIGGY STARDUST

Ziggy Stardust was a fictional character devised and brought to life by the English musician David Bowie. Although he only performed as Ziggy Stardust for 18 months in 1972–3, by the time he was 'retired' Ziggy Stardust had become the biggest phenomenon in British pop since the Beatles. According to *Rolling Stone* magazine Ziggy Stardust was the 'alter ego that changed music forever and sent his career into orbit'. The analogy was not misplaced since Ziggy Stardust had been conceived as an androgynous being from outer space who, in the creator's words, 'looked as if he had landed from Mars'. To achieve this effect Ziggy Stardust sported a flame-red mullet, shaved eyebrows and a snow-white tan. This striking appearance was teamed with a wardrobe of glamorous outfits sometimes adorned by flared leg coverings, expansive shoulder designs and bare-chested upper apparel, at others resembling the brutal functionality of the costumes worn by the dystopian gang members in Stanley Kubrick's deeply disturbing film *A Clockwork Orange*. Ziggy Stardust was a stellar success worldwide, becoming one of the iconic images of rock culture, regarded by many as the innovator's stand-out creation.

Hello, earthling.

THE THREE-DAY WEEK

The Three-day Week was one of several economic measures introduced by the Conservative government led by Edward Heath to conserve power supplies in the winter of 1973–4. These were threatened by industrial action undertaken by the labour force that extracted the coal used to generate electricity and by the railway workers who moved it around the country. There was some sympathy for the pit men, especially among those with families whose children were miners themselves. But their action had a devastating impact on the economy. The Three-day Week restricted the commercial use of this form of energy to three consecutive days. There were blackouts. Individuals had to function using torches, candles and lanterns, keeping themselves warm wrapped in blankets and duvets. Television broadcasts stopped at 10.30 in the evening, although this led to surges in demand that were only alleviated after a staggered shutdown time was introduced. Only essential consumers like hospitals, supermarkets and newspaper presses were allowed to maintain their normal usage. The Three-day Week led to a general election which saw a minority Labour administration returned to power under Harold Wilson (see page 225).

THE SWEENEY

The Sweeney was a television police drama about two officers serving in London in the 1970s. They were members of what was then called the Flying Squad (Sweeney Todd in cockney rhyming slang) who tackled hardened armed criminals. *The Sweeney* broke new ground in its small-screen depiction of British law enforcement at work. The principal characters were shown to be fallible in the way they bent rules and cut official corners as they administered their brand of justice. Using 16mm-film camera technology permitted most of the shooting to be done on location, which greatly added to the visual reality of each episode. And the degree of violence and even death marked a step change from what had been regarded as acceptable to that point. All of these, plus the high-tempo action, occasional humour and the outstanding performances of the two leads (John Thaw and Dennis Waterman), made *The Sweeney* one of the must-see shows of its era and led to a brace of feature-film spin-offs and nine books.

Nee naw nee naw nee naw...

THE GOOD LIFE

The Good Life was a television sitcom of the mid-1970s which depicted a gentle suburban idyll in marked contrast to the grainy realism of *The Sweeney.* The title is a pun on the surname of the two principal characters, Tom and Barbara Good, a couple on the cusp of middle age who reject the rat race of modern life to follow a self-sufficient lifestyle; the underlying joke being that they try to do this in the leafy environs of commuter-belt Surbiton. Next door live Margo and Jerry Leadbetter whose careful, comfortable, conventional existence is in marked contrast to the carefree quasi-bucolic chaos of their neighbours. *The Good Life* was voted ninth in a poll of best British TV comedy series and greatly advanced the careers of its four main protagonists over its run of 30 episodes spanning three years. Richard Briers (Mr Good) was already a popular comic actor, but Felicity Kendal (who played his wife), Penelope Keith (the lady in the adjacent dwelling) and Paul Eddington (her husband) all enjoyed considerable success as a result of appearing in *The Good Life.*

PUNK ROCK

Punk rock is a cylinder-shaped boiled sugar confectionery often associated with coastal resorts in Scotland – indeed locations where punk rock is sold frequently have their name cleverly printed through the length of rock from one end to the other. Enjoying punk rock is one of the enduring traditions of conventional seaside holidays.* Rock comes in a variety of colours, but a rose-coloured hue is one of the most appealing and ubiquitous. Rock of this type is usually flavoured with mint which gives its pleasing sweetness the familiar and lingering taste. The standard recipe calls for a blend of three parts sucrose to one part glucose syrup. This is brought to boiling point with water before being poured on to chilled steel plates where the golden toffee and lettering are added. Constant rolling ensures that, contrary to its name, the rock remains lump-free. As the mixture cools, counter-rotating arms steadily twist and pull it while aeration changes the colour of the sticky sweet interior substance to its distinctive white. Capital letters more commonly appear in punk rock because they are sharp, edgy and free of embellishments.

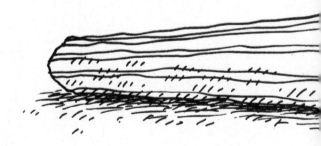

* **D** Whether deliberately, or accidentally, this author has misread the subject and set off on an interesting, though completely inaccurate discussion of 'pink rock'. To what extent this constitutes deviation, I leave the reader to decide.

THE QUEEN'S SILVER JUBILEE

The Queen's Silver Jubilee celebrated the first 25 years on the throne of Her Majesty Queen Elizabeth II. This took place in June 1977, when several days of Jubilee celebrations coincided with the Queen's official birthday. Over 12 weeks leading up to the Silver Jubilee itself, the Queen and the Duke of Edinburgh travelled widely throughout the United Kingdom, visiting 36 counties in all. They paid a Jubilee visit to Commonwealth nations later, in the autumn. There was a service of thanksgiving in St Paul's Cathedral and an estimated one million people crowded on to the Mall to see the royal family wave to onlookers. Street parties were held the length and breadth of the country. And the punk rock band the Sex Pistols performed aboard a privately chartered boat in a mockery of the Jubilee flotilla planned for 48 hours later. Their controversial rendition of 'God Save the Queen' reached number 2 in the charts and many thought it was prevented from achieving top spot through skulduggery by senior officials at the music industry's trade association.

LOUISE JOY BROWN
(THE FIRST TEST TUBE BABY)

Louise Joy Brown (the first test tube baby) made history when she was born on 25 July 1978. Not only were her parents thrilled to have given birth, their joy was made possible by a scientific breakthrough that changed the course of human reproduction. For many years Louise's mother had failed to conceive. It was only when she underwent ground-breaking treatment pioneered by clinicians Patrick Steptoe, Robert Edwards and Jean Purdy that one of her eggs was able to develop into little Louise – a feat that had begun outside her body, in a glass laboratory vessel, using the technique known as IVF (*in vitro* fertilisation), before it was placed in her uterus for the embryo to develop naturally. As the world's very first test tube baby Louise Joy Brown may have had a womb with a view, but when she and her younger sister (who had been conceived in the same way) became mothers themselves, they were able to go through the entire process in the more familiar way, relieving concerns that test tube babies might be able to fulfil their primary maternal roles conventionally.

TEST
TUBE
BABIES

mama!

OUR WINTER OF DISCONTENT

Our winter of discontent is a phrase spoken by the eponymous king in the opening line of William Shakespeare's history play *Richard III*, when he explains:

> *Now is the winter of our discontent*
> *Made glorious summer by this sun of York;*
> *And all the clouds that lour'd upon our house*
> *In the deep bosom of the ocean buried.* *

In 1979, 'our winter of discontent', the sentiment behind it was used by the editor of the *Sun* newspaper, Larry Lamb, to describe the political and social disruption that had characterised the months straddling the previous winter. Britain had been rocked by industrial unrest, and there was growing disillusionment with the Labour government led by James Callaghan, on top of which the country suffered the worst spell of bitterly cold snowy weather for 16 years. The prime minister had not helped his beleaguered position by trying to brush off the widespread resentment, which was headlined in the daily mentioned above in the memorable dismissal, 'Crisis? What crisis?'†

---

* This reference to the work of William Shakespeare is perfectly correct in this context, but it has the double benefit of using up time while also obliging others to switch their focus from Elizabethan drama to twentieth-century domestic politics, which makes keeping a check on the holy trinity of *Just A Minute* that much more difficult. Don't quote from Act V, though, where Richard tries out a bit of *epanalepsis*, where the words that begin a sentence also end it. It's the famous line decrying his horselessness.

† **R** Repetition – but as the whistle blew! Always worth a try.

A TIMELINE OF THE 1980s...

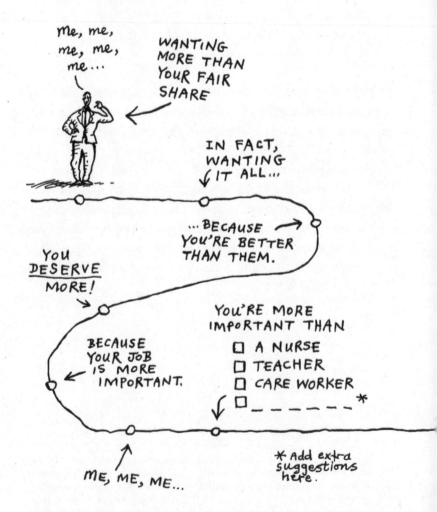

21

The 1980s

ME.

ME.

AND EVEN IF YOUR
JOB ISN'T MORE
IMPORTANT, WHO
CARES? LIFE AIN'T
FAIR...

Etcetera...

MY MEMORIES OF MARGARET THATCHER

Margaret Hilda Thatcher, née Roberts, later Baroness Thatcher, a Lady of the Garter, a member of the Order of Merit, leader of the Conservative Party for 15 years from 1975, the longest-serving prime minister of the twentieth century and the first woman to hold that office – and I was lucky enough to know her! And, amazingly, our founder chairman Nicholas Parsons's dad was a GP in Grantham a century ago and was the man who brought Margaret Thatcher into the world. Whichever way you look at the history of Britain, *Just A Minute* is part of the story. And whatever your politics, you have to acknowledge her achievement as the nation's premier female PM. There was only one downside to Mrs Thatcher – she had no sense of humour, none whatsoever. I always thought that must have made bringing up her son, Mark, quite a challenge. Famously, when her speechwriters gave her a parody of the 'dead parrot' joke to use in a party conference speech, she queried it, saying, 'I don't understand it.' 'Trust us,' they replied, 'It's from Monty Python. It's very funny. The audience will love it.' 'This Monty Python,' said Thatcher unconvinced, 'is he one of us?'*

---

* **R** Yes, there is a repetition of 'Monty Python' there, but sometimes you have got to risk it for the sake of the story.

SIR CLIVE SINCLAIR

Once upon a time, what a name to reckon with! Sir Clive Sinclair was awarded his knighthood in 1983 for his contributions to the UK's personal computing industry, the market in which the Sinclair brand at its peak commanded 45 per cent of the turnover. These days that trade is dominated by big international manufacturers like Apple, Dell, HP – Hewlett Packard, not the sauce – and Sony, but back in the day the devices made by Clive Sinclair's companies occupied a mighty chunk of home sales, setting a trend for IT innovation, and later video entertainment, in both of which this country continues to excel.* At the very start of the decade that forms the chronological theme† of this section, he released his first PC, the Sinclair ZX80, which cost under £100. Its success was followed by later models that became popular in Europe and in the USA. Sinclair machines proved to be especially liked by users who enjoyed playing games on them, a trend that grew and expanded after the name Sinclair had faded from prominence. He went on to design tiny cars and a bicycle that you could fold up and keep in your handbag.

Brum brum brum...

* It would be churlish to challenge during a proud patriotic assertion like this.

† **R** Nice way to introduce a timeline that avoids repetition of both 'nineteen' and 'eighty'.

WELCOMING THE WORLD WIDE WEB

Welcoming the World Wide Web is something that I did with enthusiasm after Tim Berners-Lee created the first website in 1989. The internet has given us email, Facebook, and funny cat videos. The World Wide Web has also brought a new vocabulary to enrich our language. Two decades ago few of these would have been widely used, whereas today our lives would be incomplete without terms like: app, attachment, avatar, bandwidth, bitcoin, blog, broadband, browser, byte, chat, cloud, cookie, cursor, cyberspace, database, default, domain, download, emoji, encryption, firewall, freeware, Grindr, hacker, HTML, hyperlink, icon, intranet, IP address, ISP, hashtag, malware, meme, menu bar, netiquette, netizen, network, noob, password, PDF, phishing, platform, plug and play, port, protocol, RAM, router, search engine, selfie, sexting, silver surfer, Snapchat, social media, spam, spreadsheet, streaming, spyware, Tinder, troll, tweet, unfriend, upload vine, USB drive, user ID, video conferencing, viral, virus, virtual memory, webcam, web hosting, webpage, Windows, wi-fi and wireless. There's no question that in welcoming the World Wide Web we changed not just the way we communicate but how we interact with the world at large. Snail mail anyone?*

---

* Over half the entry is devoted to words and phrases connected to the World Wide Web. There's no deviation, repetition, nor hesitation – just a lot of memory and possibly a degree of bewilderment about what some of it actually means.

DELIA SMITH

Who is Delia? What is she? Delia Smith is a cook and television presenter who became the first superstar of the kitchen through teaching several generations of British people to prepare food in a more adventurous yet no-nonsense way. For example, she suggests two ways to boil an egg. There's the one I regard as the intense method, which requires concentration, something called simmering and the complicated use of a saucepan lid. Option B is more straightforward: bung the *oeuf* – as the French chefs call it – into a pan of cold water, bring it to boiling point and then keep going until you reckon it's going to be well enough done for your liking. With book sales extending well beyond 20 million, Delia Smith knows what she's writing about. When her *Winter Collection* was published it accounted for one tenth of the retail book market, making it one of the best-selling cookery titles of all time. The 'Delia effect' extended to supermarkets too, where the eggs apparently leapt 10 per cent in popularity following one of her TV shows. Delia Smith once caused a national shortage of cranberries when fresh fruit shelves were swept clear by customers clamouring to recreate a recipe she had been demonstrating.

CHANNEL 4

Channel 4 is a free-to-air public service television network in Britain which began transmission on 2 November 1982. At 16.45 that day the first episode of *Countdown* inaugurated the new channel and that popular show has now notched up over 7000 episodes and is still going strong, I'm pleased to say, since I have taken part in its proceedings more than a few times. However, my association with Channel 4 has not been restricted to that lexico-graphical gem. Moving outside the studio, I accompanied Sheila Hancock on a series of *Great Canal Journeys* on which we explored Britain by narrowboat. We began in London before moving to Staffordshire, the Cambridgeshire fens, west Lancashire, our old haunts in Stratford-upon-Avon and the Peak District. Working for Channel 4 was not without its hazards. I took a towpath tumble while we were filming, but my kind co-host revived me with a cup of tea and I survived to carry on with the show, even if one side of my face looked as if I'd just been knocked out of the ring by Tyson Fury.*

---

* **D** You might be tempted to challenge for deviation, given this diversion into the author's personal experiences. However, a strong rebuttal could be mounted on the grounds that everything related here is directly connected to Channel 4 and therefore cleaves to the subject rather than cleaving from it.

GRANGE HILL

Grange Hill was a TV series that ran for exactly 30 years as part of the British Broadcasting Corporation's programming for children. Only, some of the storylines and depiction of life and learning in the comprehensive school Grange Hill gave viewers a very different look at contemporary education compared with many of the programmes that had gone before. The creators of *Grange Hill* set out to eradicate what they saw as 'the Enid Blyton, middle-class' drama that had permeated television aimed at younger audiences to that point. Instead, *Grange Hill* tackled storylines about issues such as drug addition, racism, child abuse, teenage pregnancy, mental illness, homelessness, gun crime, alcoholism and death. But this approach was too edgy by far for senior executives and the *Grange Hill* creators faced the threat of having their show pulled from the airwaves unless they moderated the scripts and eased back on the most controversial stuff. Even though they complied, *Grange Hill* still achieved a huge following, with its last airing having an audience of half a million.

THE NEW ROMANTICS

'The New Romantics' was a term coined for followers of a fashion-cum-music trend that flourished briefly at the start of the 1980s. The New Romantics had previously been known by a variety of other terms such as: new dandies, romantic rebels and the Blitz Kids. As a reaction to the anti-fash stance of punk rock, the New Romantics adopted fashions drawn from an eclectic mix of eras and influences ranging from late eighteenth-century Romanticism, to cabaret costumes of the thirties. The use of synthesisers characterised much of the work of New Romantic bands like Spandau Ballet, Visage and Duran-say-it-again. They found particular success in the USA where British artists dominated the charts for a period, when approaching one in three records sold were by performers from the UK, who at one point also accounted for six of the top ten hits. Commentators regard the Live Aid concert in the middle of the decade as the high-water mark for the New Romantic performers. Revivals were attempted in later years, but they never achieved the same level of popularity and influence as the old New Romantics.

MONEY

Why did the woman put her money in her freezer? Because she wanted some cold, hard cash. *Money*, or *Money: A Suicide Note* to give it its full title, is a work by Martin Amis that has been hailed as the defining tale of its era. A commentator in the *Guardian* described *Money* as 'a neo-Rabelaisian comedy … a zeitgeist book that remains one of the dominant novels of the 1980s', while the *Spectator* identified it as 'an epitaph to that decade'. *Money* is a comic satire of the conspicuous consumerism that characterised the period. At its centre stands John Self, who careers about on four wheels in a car aptly named Fiasco and adopts the same approach to everything else in his life. Excess is the protagonist's guiding principle whether in food and drink, drugs and debauchery, or whatever else catches his fancy – because in *Money* money* is all anyone needs providing that it comes in limitless sums. However, money is shown to be as much a corrupting influence as a creative one and the writer refers more than once in his narrative to money by the term he uses for his subtitle.†

Money is like fairies... It only exists because we believe in it.

---

* **R** This is of course acceptable repetition in a way that the ABBA song title (see Offa's Dyke on page 18) is not.

† **R** Smart use of the subject title wording to repeat the word 'money' in a variety of contexts, particularly as consecutive words: book title and noun.

SHAPARAK KHORSANDI ON ...
LADETTES

The 'Ladettes' were a nineties phenomenon where young women, myself included, threw themselves into a culture of binge drinking and emulating the worst of what had been traditionally 'Lad' behaviour. Ladettes were 'taking the power back!' mostly by vomiting in our own hair and losing our shoes on the night bus. Yes. We were the generation who muddled 'feminism' up with 'alcoholism'. 'HE'S having ten pints! WHY can't I?' I would belligerently cry, pointing at a gargantuan rugby player. A kind friend pointed out, 'Because you are five foot two, you'd die,' which was fair enough. The Ladette decade helped give rise to the Spice Girls who epitomised what it was to be a Ladette, putting your mates before a boyfriend, speaking your mind and offering Liam Gallagher out for a fight, as Sporty did in a 1997 speech at the Brit Awards. She yelled out to him, 'Come and have a go if you think you're hard enough.' As an ex-Ladette, I am in awe of Gen Zedders now who don't seem to think regularly waking up on a pavement outside G.A.Y. means you are having fun. They see it more as mark of mental health issues that need to be addressed. The youth of today uses words like 'selfcare' ... for us Ladettes, this just meant having a Berocca and a morning-after pill.

whose round is it?

THE M25

I heard a report on the news that a maniac was driving the wrong way around the M25. I called my dad to warn him because he was due to drive over to see me. He answered from the car: 'There's not just one, son, there's hundreds of them.' The M25 is a 117-mile-long road that encircles Greater London. The idea of an orbital motorway around the capital had been proposed early in the twentieth century but it took until the seventies for concrete plans to be put in place and construction to begin. The new road was very popular at first. Coach tours were laid on to convey passengers around its full circumference; amazingly, some were still operating as recently as a couple of decades ago. In the general election held in the year following the inauguration of the M25, Margaret Thatcher's Conservative Party won every constituency through which the M25 passed. However, its popularity quickly led to congestion, which bred a slew of negative jokes, the most familiar being the description of the M25 as the largest car park in Britain. Carriageway widening has alleviated some of the worst pinch points but the M25 remains one of the busiest thoroughfares in Europe, in places carrying as many as 196,000 vehicles a day.

EASTENDERS

Dirty Den? Peggy Mitchell? Tiffany Butcher? Do the names ring a bell? Of course, they do. They are characters from *EastEnders*, the soap opera that has been aired by the Beeb on its number One channel since 1985. It was created in response to the need for the network to attract the kind of consistently large audiences that were tuning in to watch *Coronation Street* (see page 235) on its rival, ITV. As the name implies, *EastEnders* is set in the working-class area of London's East End. The specific location is the fictitious Albert Square in the equally fictional* borough of Walford, where the daily lives of typical families rooted in that part of the capital are followed as they confront and adapt to the social and economic changes of modern life. From its outset, *EastEnders* set out to portray a grainier, grittier realism in its characterisation and storylines than had been the case in similar series. It also included pets. I seem to remember a dog called Wellard. And Sharon had a pet poodle named Roly, as I recall. Lady Di is the current canine on the screen, played by a pooch whose real name is Hot Lips, I believe. Seventeen and a third million viewers tuned in to the first episode and *EastEnders* continues to return the most consistent ratings of any television programme transmitted by the corporation.

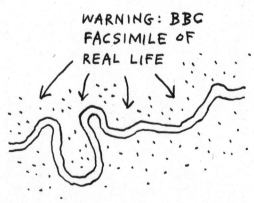

WARNING: BBC
FACSIMILE OF
REAL LIFE

---

* **R** Cheeky move to avoid the repetition of 'fictitious' by replacing it with 'fictional'.

22

Cool Britannia

THE PREMIER LEAGUE

Name three Premier League teams that contain rude words. Arsenal, Scunthorpe and effing Man United? Actually, one of them isn't in the Premier League – a soccer set-up established in 1992 in which 20 clubs compete, with the leading one at the end of the season being crowned its champion while the bottom three are relegated from the Premier League to the Championship, a tier below. Football in this country had been in decline in the second half of the eighties. Banned from European competition for five years following the Heysel Stadium disaster, with a number of leading players going abroad to further their careers, falling attendances and facilities in dire need of investment, the top ones got together and planned a breakaway competition to generate greater revenue and raise the standard of the national game to match that played in leading continental countries such as Italy's Serie A and La Liga in Spain. When the Premier League was inaugurated its members were: the A team already mentioned, Aston Villa, Blackburn Rovers, Chelsea, Coventry City, Crystal Palace, Everton, Ipswich Town, Leeds, Liverpool, the two from near Salford, Middlesborough, Norwich,* Nottingham Forest, Oldham Athletic, Queens Park Rangers, Sheffields Wednesday and Unified,† Southampton, Tottenham Hotspur and Wimbledon. Since then the Premier League has been largely dominated by six of those listed.

---

* **R** Apologies to the Canaries and their many fans. The official name of the club is, of course, Norwich City. But to avoid repetition, 'City' can only be used once and, in accordance with alphabetical order, it has had to go to Coventry. Similar apologies are due to Manchester United and its followers.

† **R** Same issue, different solution – and a felicitous one as it happens. At a glance, Unified and United look strikingly and orthographically similar.

MR BLOBBY

Mr Blobby was one of those curiously British confections that enjoyed his relatively brief spell in the limelight before sinking from public life into almost total obscurity, dismissed by a national paper as one of the '10 most irritating television characters ever'. But in some respects Mr Blobby represented the nation's mood searching for madcap relief and escapism early in the new decade which wanted to turn its back on the drab 1980s. Mr Blobby was not the most physically prepossessing newcomer to prime-time TV. A bloated pink individual covered in yellow spots, with grin jiggly eyes and a fixed toothy grin, he communicated by way of a one-word vocabulary 'Blobby'. At the peak of his fame Mr Blobby's Christmas song entitled (you guessed it) 'Blobby' occupied the number one spot for three weeks confirming, as the *New York Times* suggested, that Mr Blobby was, 'a metaphor for a nation gone soft in the head. Others have seen him as proof of Britain's deep-seated attraction to trash.' To which the inevitable riposte has to be, 'Blobby!'

BLOBBY!

— BLOBBY...

—BLOBBY! *

* Help! Help!
Get me out...
I'm trapped in
this costume...

THE CHANNEL TUNNEL

The Channel Tunnel opened in 1994 and for the first time since Britain became an island about 8000 years ago (see first entry in this book) the country had a fixed link with the European mainland. The present Channel Tunnel was not the earliest on the drawing board. Plans to dig a tunnel connecting northern France with southeast England cropped up periodically throughout the nineteenth century. The two World Wars of the first half of the twentieth dampened enthusiasm a bit, but once the UK was part of the Common Market, then the double-E-C and what became the European Union, work began in earnest; although there were sceptics on both sides of the Channel. 'Why do French people look so depressed?' ran one enquiry, to which the answer was 'Because the light at the end of the tunnel is Folkestone.' On our side, deep-rooted suspicions of 'Johnny foreigner' were aired in doggerel such as:

> There'll be carloads of Louises
> There'll be Swedes of charmless candour
> From Parisian stripteases
> Coming over to philander,
> Importing foul diseases
> Spreading left-wing propaganda
> Into Kent.

NEW LABOUR

New Labour was a slogan adopted by the Labour Party in Britain which appeared in 1994. It marked a shift in Labour emphasis to embrace market economics and ditch one of the long-standing Labour tenets, Clause IV of the Labour constitution, which demanded common ownership of industry. New Labour ideology permeated the Labour hierarchy from the mid-1990s until 2010, under the leadership of Tony Blair and Gordon Brown. After that, New Labour fell from favour and was widely reviled among left-wing factions: the anagram of Tony Blair MP is 'I'm Tory plan B'! The spirit of New Labour* was rich material for satirists. Here's one New Labour version of the socialist anthem, 'L'Internationale':

The People's Flag is salmon pink,
It's not as red as you might think.
White collar workers come and cheer
The Labour leader once a year.

So raise the umbrella high,
The bowler hat, the old school tie.
So people think we're still sincere,
We'll sing the Red Standard† once a year.

* **R** As summed up in the three-word soundbite which would, in *Just A Minute* terms, be rendered 'Education'.

† **R** The correct rendition should, of course, read 'Flag' to repeat the opening line. But since this is a repetition 'Standard' has been used instead to avoid a challenge.

TONY AND CHERIE

Tony and Cherie are the first names of Tony Blair and Cherie Booth, the British politician and his wife who lived in 10 Downing Street for a decade from 1997, during which they raised a family while he ran the country and she practised law; their fourth child, Leo, was the first legitimate offspring born to a serving United Kingdom prime minister for more than 150 years and is believed to have been conceived while the premier and his lady were visiting the Queen and the Duke of Edinburgh at Balmoral. Tony and Cherie were viewed by many as the embodiment of New Labour (see page 273). They also championed the notion of Cool Britannia (coming shortly), inviting celebrities from the worlds of rock music, fashion and the arts to receptions in their official residence. On the world stage Tony and Cherie hobnobbed with heads of state and government, which critics imply may have fuelled the couple's over-inflated self-opinions, often recounted in jokes like the one in which Tony slips on the wet floor after getting out of his bath. 'Mon Dieu!' exclaims Cherie. The PM slowly gets up and says: 'How many times do I have to tell you, Cherie? At home, you may call me Tony.'

COOL BRITANNIA

Cool Britannia is an anagram of 'Blair no action'; it's also a name given to an era of resurgent pride in UK culture (particularly when applied to activities popular with the youthful segment of the population), which coincided with the early years of the aforementioned politician's spell as prime minister. After the, to some, dispiriting decades of the seventies and eighties, improving economic conditions coupled with the international success of Britpop musicians such as Oasis, Blur and the Spice Girls (of whom more shortly) generated a sense of confidence that infused national life to the point that everything that seemed significant was bright, brash and British. It was also edgy. Artists won renown for pickling sharks or forgetting to make the bed. For the first time since the Swinging Sixties, London was seen as the style capital of the world, a position that was confirmed when the US magazine *Vanity Fair* published a 25-page special called 'London Swings Again'. But the phenomenon of Cool Britannia iced over when the artistes that provided its soundtrack were replaced by the next wave.

SHAPARAK KHORSANDI ON ...
ALTERNATIVE COMEDY

I was twelve when what became known as alternative comedy came along in the eighties, blowing away the cobwebbed, besuited blokes doing mother-in-law jokes and instead poking fun at the establishment. Ben Elton, Rik Mayall, Alexei Sayle and Lise Mayer wrote *The Young Ones*, an anarchic sitcom about four students, which horrified po-faced adults but us kids adored it. It was the closest thing my generation had to punk and this TV programme, in many ways, defined my coming of age. These young comedians were 'politically correct', which back then just meant you weren't a racist, sexist homophobe. They riled the po-faced grown-ups, which made their world intoxicating to me. Julian Clary was also at the forefront of alternative comedy. An out gay person, exquisitely made-up, making no apology for who he was, a wild thing in those days. I remember watching him on a TV phone-in when a mother complained, 'My kids see you and are confused, "Is he a man or a woman?" and I tell them I don't know.' Quick as a flash, his reply came back: 'Well, I think that's you messing them up, not me.' Jo Brand, with her red lips and DM boots, stuck two fingers up at convention, smashed up the barriers and paved a path for myriad other female comics to follow.

DEVOLUTION

Devolution, the process by which central government delegates power to a lower level authority, often a regional assembly, has occupied British domestic politics for much of the last century. The first significant act of devolution took place in Ireland when the 26 counties of southern Eire became an independent country, leaving the remaining area of the north as a member of the United Kingdom, but with its own parliament. England is now the only one of the home nations not to have a devolved assembly, although there are growing calls from various quarters, especially in Cornwall and Yorkshire. These have been driven in part by the creation in the late 1990s of the Scottish Parliament and the Senedd in Wales.* Both of these were established to deliver a greater degree of local autonomy in the way things were run. However, the powers granted through devolution do not amount to full independence and it is this which is driving political parties like the SNP and Plaid Cymru in their bids for absolute freedom to do it their own way, free of control from Westminster. This minute isn't rich in chuckles, is it? But then Mark Drakeford and Nicola Sturgeon, two of the leading lights of the devolved territories, are neither of them known as natural rib-ticklers. (Apparently, in private they're both huge fun, but I've never got that close.)

---

* **R** Because some hold that they are distinct words, you could try getting away with something like 'Senedd, the Welsh senate,' but the tactic might be *peryglus*, or indeed perilous.

MANCHESTER

Manchester hasn't always had the best billing. 'Play a real life version of *Grand Theft Auto*,' went a typical cheap gag, 'and spend a day in Manchester.' But derogatory attitudes began to change with the arrival of the last decades of the twentieth century during which Manchester was transformed into a cultural hub pulsating with the innovative sounds of bands like Oasis, the Stone Roses, Happy Mondays, Inspiral Carpets, James, the Charlatans and 808 State, which radiated nationwide and then globally. Behind many of them was Tony Wilson (aka 'Mr Manchester'), founder of Factory Records and the legendary Haçienda club. It was he who is also credited with coining the term 'Madchester' to describe the increasingly popular draw of indie dance and indie rave which characterised the new and refreshing music generated by Manchester-based groups. At the same time, at Old Trafford, a group of hopeful young football players were beginning to make their mark at Manchester United by winning the 1992 FA Youth Cup – among them hopefuls like Ryan Giggs and David Beckham. You may have heard of them. I have.

THE SPICE GIRLS

The Spice Girls were a British girl group at the forefront of the teen pop momentum of the 1990s. There were five members of the Spice Girls – not to be confused with the earlier US artistes Salt-N-Pepa – who prophesied 'girl power' and reached number one in the charts in 36 countries with their debut single 'Wannabe'. This success was followed by their first album *Spice*, which sold 23 million copies around the world, the highest figures ever achieved by an all-female ensemble. Advertising deals and endorsements followed and although the Spice Girls parted at the end of the millennium to pursue independent careers, their global income had made them one of the most lucrative marketing machines in history. Although the Spice Girls may have become Old Spice, by the time they split they had established themselves as the most widely recognised troupe of popular musicians since the Beatles (see page 16). Their popularity endured and when they were reunited at the closing ceremony of London's 2012 Olympics their performance became the most tweeted moment of the entire competition.

HARRY POTTER

Harry Potter is the name of a boy wizard created by J.K. Rowling as the central character in a series of seven fantasy novels, the first of which was published in 1997.* *Harry Potter and the Philosopher's Stone*, number one in the Harry Potter canon, was famously rejected a dozen times by commercial book producers before one decided to take a chance on it. And then it was only because the publisher's young daughter wanted to find out what happened at the end. It proved to be a good call. Global sales of the Harry Potter titles have made it the best-selling story sequence in history. On top of that, the narrative has been turned into eight feature films, and total income from all Harry Potter spin-offs is reckoned to be in the order of $25 billion – not a bad return for an author who famously wrote some of initial manuscript in cafés. Now, here's a question for Potterheads: how many Harry Potters does it take to screw in a lightbulb? Answer: two – one to hold the illumination device, and one to rotate the room.

---

* **H** Hagrid is so terrified when telling Harry about Voldemort that he lapses into both anadiplosis and epanalepsis: 'See, there was this wizard who went … bad. As bad as you could go. Worse. Worse than worse.'

23

The New Millennium

THE MILLENNIUM DOME

The Millennium Dome is now called the O2, no doubt to the relief of many who oversaw its first incarnation. *The Times* voiced a general mood of disapproval and disappointment about what was intended to be Britain's principal national 'statement' heralding the third millennium when it observed, 'The Millennium Dome was a gigantic, surreal, Ruritanian folly. It made Tony Blair look like a reincarnation of Mad King Ludwig. For a mere £1 billion, he gave the British people a tent filled with nothing in particular in a forgotten, inaccessible part of London.'* On paper the Dome looked well-conceived. Located very close to the Greenwich meridian, denominations of time were represented symbolically by its 12 supporting towers and 365-metre diameter. The problems lay in a gross overestimate of visitor numbers. The Dome was open throughout the year 2000; when only slightly over half the expected number turned up, it showed a deficit of over 200 million smackers. Ironically, it's now a hugely successful music venue, which earned its new owners in just a decade as much as the Millennium Dome had lost the taxpayer.

---

* Smart use of a quotation, completely on message and therefore totally legitimate for *Just A Minute*.

JAMIE OLIVER

Jamie Oliver is a cook, proprietor of a chain of eateries and recipe-book author who appeared during the first decade of this millennium as the cheery, cheeky face of TV commercials for the Sainsbury's supermarket chain. Jamie Oliver was always destined to be a chef. His parents ran a pub/restaurant and he has five ingredients in his name: jam, oil, olive, liver and mie. (Eh? Apparently, it's a variety of noodle.)* Jamie's laid-back, easy style on camera was first spotted when he made an unscripted contribution to a documentary about the River Café in Fulham. That led to the commissioning of his own debut show *The Naked Chef* and the writing of his first cookery publication, which became a bestseller. Jamie's Italian opened its first premises in 2008 and 41 others followed at home and overseas before the group hit serious financial problems after ten years of trading as its heyday pasta way, after it ran out of thyme and its legacy became a pizza history – proving that even a celebrity chef cannoli do so much.†

---

* That's good – adding extra words from the subject's own name. It also sets others off on a tangent trying to work out what's going on. Divide and rule (in every sense) is the name of the game on *Just A Minute*.

† Punning down to the finish – the hallmark of a seasoned practitioner of the art of metonymical circumlocution.

POSH AND BECKS

Posh and Becks are the media nicknames for Victoria and David Beckham. As a member of the hugely successful all-female group described earlier (see page 279), the former was given the moniker Posh Spice. Her husband is a footballer who played for Manchester United, Real Madrid, LA Galaxy and Paris St Germain, as well as having loan spells with Preston North End and AC Milan. On the international scene, he captained the England team and won 115 caps. So, Posh and Becks had all the credentials to become cultural icons and as a celebrity super-couple they have raised four children and still stayed married to each other, which has not escaped comment. Some are surprised that Posh remains with Becks, because they never saw him as a keeper. The way they chose to call their offspring has been much remarked on too. 'You know who really gives kids a bad name?' ran an award-winning gag at the Edinburgh Fringe, 'Posh and Becks.' And Shakespeare aficionados enjoy the one about their second son who asked his football coach, 'What shirt am I?' to be told, 'Wear four out there, Romeo.'

BIG BROTHER

Big Brother is a television reality competition in which a group of contestants, referred to as 'housemates', live together in a domestic setting, cut off from the outside world – like lockdown, but with more laughs (one hopes) and the same level of mounting tension. To add to the merriment, those taking part in *Big Brother* are under constant scrutiny 24/7 from hidden cameras and personal microphones. Over the duration of the programme, the number of participants is gradually whittled down as individuals are evicted by being voted out. The one left at the end becomes the winner and receives a cash prize. This formula proved to be an enormous hit with British viewers from the moment the initial episode aired in July 2000. Over the 18 years that it was broadcast, *Big Brother* turned some of its contenders into minor celebrities, while those whose day job was being an actual celebrity were given a *Big Brother* production all to themselves. Attentive readers of this book may recall that we have encountered Big Brother earlier in our survey of national history. In case you missed it, revisit George Orwell's *1984* (see page 200).

THE GREAT BRITISH BAKE OFF

The Great British Bake Off is a reference attentive readers may also record from earlier in this book (see page 21). It's a television competition programme in which amateur contestants vie with each other to impress judges with the quality of their baking. At the end of each round, one of them is eliminated and the winner is chosen from those who make it through to the final edition of the series. As an entertainment employing the vocabulary of the kitchen, pantry and oven, *The Great British Bake Off* is rich in double entendres and cheeky innuendos occasioned by the use of words like: balls, baps and buns. Bottoms crop up quite a bit in unfortunate associations, regularly being described as: soggy, sweaty and exposed. Others are even more arresting, but even though *The Great British Bake Off* began as a production for the British Broadcasting Corporation, I think it would be safer not to venture further down this prurient path.* On the up side, the National Federation of Women's Institutes reported that the popularity of *The Great British Bake Off* prompted its greatest surge in membership since the release of the film *Calendar Girls*.

---

* **D** Very clever diversion which appears to veer towards deviation but avoids the dreaded challenge, sticking just close enough to the subject to ward one off.

FOOT AND MOUTH

The Foot in Mouth award is an annual honour inaugurated by the Plain English Campaign and presented for 'a baffling comment by a public figure'.* The first to be celebrated was former US Vice President Dan Quayle, a past master of the unintelligible and vacuous. He received a post-dated Foot in Mouth accolade for this memorable 1991 gem: 'We offer the party as a big tent. How we do that with the platform, the preamble to [it]† or whatnot, that remains to be seen. But that message will have to be articulated with great clarity.' Exactly – I think. He was followed by Gordon Brown three years later, after the then Shadow Chancellor of the Exchequer held forth earnestly on 'New Economics' by way of impenetrable jargon such as: 'the expansion of post neo-classical endogenous growth theory'. And Boris Johnson enjoyed his moment of glory with the 2004 Foot in Mouth for the line, 'I could not fail to disagree with you less', which he delivered, rather felicitously, on the TV show *Have I Got News for You*.

* **D** The author has once again misread the topic. The subject should be the foot-and-mouth disease, which affects cloven-hoofed animals. However, with word 'disease' missing, a possible misreading has led to a discourse on the more light-hearted topic of the awards described. In these circumstances a challenge for deviation might be lodged, but you can't be said to be deviating from the topic if you never got started on it in the first place!

† **R** Vice President Quayle actually repeated the word 'platform' at this point, but the author has substituted the word 'it' to avoid a challenge for repetition.

THE LONDON OLYMPICS

The London Olympics were first held in 1908. It was another 40 years before they were held in the UK capital for a second time and the most recent London Olympics took place in 2012. Readers may remember my earlier remarks about the Olympics, but in spite any personal sentiments, the London Olympics (officially the Games of the XXX Olympiad) were hailed as a huge success — not simply because of the outstanding performance of Team GB (which finished third in the medal table), but also for how they were stage-managed and presented. I'm referring, of course, to the two movie sequences that featured in the opening ceremony when Her Majesty the Queen took a leading role as a Bond babe in Danny Boyle's 007 spectacular *Happy & Glorious* and Rowan Atkinson's Mr Bean (see page 242) triumphed in what you might call a rerun of the Oscar-winning Olympic film *Chariots of Fire*. Boris Johnson got in the act as well, of course, practically upstaging our first gold medal by getting stuck on a zip wire to promote Olympic attractions while sporting a hard hat and waving a couple of plastic Union Jacks.

MO FARAH

Mo Farah is the most successful British track athlete in modern Olympic history. As a long-distance competitor, he won the gold medal in both the men's 5000- and 10,000-metre events at successive Olympiads: London 2012 and in Rio de Janeiro four years later. With ten global titles, Mo Farah is the most decorated competitor in the annals of GB athletics. Since May of the year when London last staged the games, Mo Farah has celebrated his wins with a movement and gesture called the Mobot. The idea was suggested during an episode of the TV panel show *A League of Their Own* when the host James Corden invited contestants to devise a dance to mark Mo's wins. Clare Balding came up with the one that has stuck, a hand motion to represent the letter that follows L in the alphabet, taking her inspiration from the dance to the hit by the Village People, 'YMCA'. A year after his twin victories in Brazil, Mo Farah was awarded a knighthood in the Queen's New Year Honours list for services to his sport.

COALITION GOVERNMENT

Coalition government is not something that occurs very much in the UK. However, in 2010 a coalition government was formed between the Conservative Party led by David Cameron and the Liberal Democrats whose leader was Nick Clegg. Contrary to widespread expectations this coalition government lasted five years during which the economy was strengthened, pensioners were given full control of their retirement pots, education was shaken up and same-sex marriages acquired legal status. Against these, the debit side chalked up the chaotic intervention in Libya, which removed Gaddafi but left the country in a political vacuum; the 'Omnishambles' budget two years into the programme which many took as a sign that Chancellor of the Exchequer George Osborne was losing his grip; the failure to implement any constitutional reforms because of bickering between the coalition partners; flip-flopping over EU membership; and uncertainty about Scottish independence. When it came to an end fifteen years into the twenty-first century the larger party (the Tories) secured their first outright win in 23 years, but their former partners lost all but 8 of their 57 MPs. Who cares about politics anyway?

WILLIAM AND KATE

William and Kate are the first names of a forty-something couple who graduated from University of St Andrews in 2005: to wit William Wales and Catherine Middleton – although he was referred to as Steve by fellow students. William had been brought up in the family home in London, Kate in her parents' abode to the west down the M4 at Bucklebury, in Berkshire. She finished her schooling at Marlborough College, where she was captain of the girls' hockey team. He went to a different one, just over the river from his grandmother's home at Windsor. They got to know each other as undergraduates after Kate had caught William's eye at a charity fashion show where she modelled a see-through lace dress. When that was sold at auction, nine years later, the buyer had to stump up £78,000 in total. But this Kate M was not destined to follow that other celebrated Kate (Ms Moss) down a professional career as a queen of the catwalk. Although she knew she would have to wait before being 'crowned', she was also aware that once it happened hers would be a long-term engagement.

POSSIBLE WAYS FORWARD
FROM HERE...

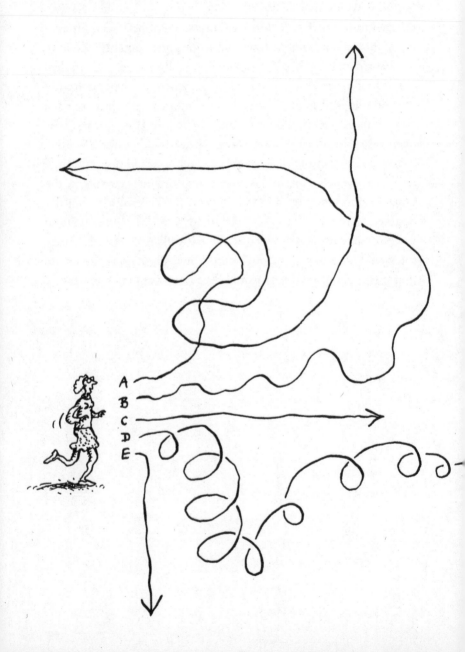

24

Here and Now

POP!

LIVING IN THE HERE AND NOW

Living in the here and now? I don't find it easy. I am not comfortable in the twenty-first century. I don't want to learn another frigging password. And I don't want to know what's going out there in the real world. Am I alone? I often find that what I am doing turns out to be what the rest of the world is doing, too. I am not watching, reading, tuning in to the news any more. Perhaps T. S. Eliot was right and 'Humankind cannot bear very much reality.' I gave up on the *Today* programme a while ago. Who wants hectoring at breakfast? It must be 18 months since I last watched the *News at Ten* – and I count Huw Edwards as a friend. On radio I only listen to *Just A Minute* – and the Shipping Forecast. On TV I only watch *Bargain Hunt* – and *Homes Under the Hammer*. And *Naked Attraction*. The result of this self-imposed global information blackout is that I am less informed but much happier. I pick up the gist of what is going on around our beleaguered planet in passing, but I am not getting bogged down in the depressing detail. As a consequence, I am having a very merry time – thank you for asking. Triple jabbed and masked I am out and about day and night as if there's no tomorrow. Perhaps there is no tomorrow? I wouldn't know.*

---

* **R** Another daring repetition for rhetorical effect. Let's give him the benefit of the doubt. After all, today, who does know if there will be a tomorrow?

BREXIT

Brexit (which would have been so much popular if they'd called it 'The Great British Break Off') is one of those strange national tics we British seem to go in for. Everything can be jogging along reasonably well and then we lob a spanner in the works. As readers of this book may now be aware, our relationship with European neighbours has had its ups and downs throughout history. Would-be Brexiteers didn't react well when Julius Caesar (remember him?) extended his holiday in France to see what it was like this side of the Channel. A millennium later early medieval Brexiteers got shirty when the Normans imposed their own form of Eurocentric control. Our trouble is that this country fared OK when our continental chums were in charge back then. We had an early shot at Brexit after problems with the Spanish Armada and bust-ups with the French and the Dutch. But we ended up at each other's throats in civil war and it took an orange purveyor from the Netherlands and then a German farming family to straighten things out again.* But Brexit promised the chance to think big, so maybe we should set about reversing historical setbacks, starting with the aim to 'Make America Great Britain' again.

* **D** A good example of appearing to follow the rules while actually holding forth on subjects which are, at best, tangential to the topic. But, by inserting a key word (in this case the topic itself, 'Brexit') you can forestall challenges for deviation.

SNOWFLAKES

Why are some people in favour of global warming? Because they want all the snowflakes to disappear forever! Snowflakes are a remarkable phenomenon of nature and of our times. They present themselves as cool and unique – astonishingly no two are alike, or so popular opinion would have us believe – although they frequently turn out to be nothing more than simply cold and seriously flaky. But snowflakes catch public attention by suddenly appearing on the scene, frequently causing a great deal of disruption to others, before melting away never to be seen again. Snowflakes are also desperately fragile. Try to examine them too closely and they crumble and dissolve. Historically snowflakes come in various formations. Snowflakes used to be found gathering in drifts. This led some folk to dig what they were doing, while others simply wanted to clear the way ahead by blowing the snowflakes aside. The point is we have real snowflakes – as in the riddle, 'What is a snowman's favourite cereal? Snowflakes' – and the other kind: over-sensitive souls who bleat 'If someone calls me a snowflake one more time, I'm going into meltdown.'

SNOWFLAKES MELTING

NAKED ATTRACTION

Naked attraction is both a well-established turn of phrase and the title of an extraordinary television show that I have only seen by chance when staying on my own in a lonely hotel and flicking through the channels looking for *Newsnight*. In a nutshell, *Naked Attraction* is a dating show where contestants pick potential partners entirely on the basis of what they look like without their clothes on – yes, starkers, in the nuddy, in the altogether, with their kit off and their bits on full display. I am not making this up. There are a lot of close-ups, so you don't miss a thing. The episode I caught featured a man named Ian who, at 75, was the programme's oldest contestant to date: trim, toned, and, as he showed us, sporting a fine Prince Albert on his todger – or winky, as the charming receptionist who had joined me to watch preferred to term it. She'd kindly brought up some extra teabags because I'd run out. Anyway, this old codger on *Naked Attraction* told us that he'd been 30 years a happily married man, and straight, but in his widower-hood he wanted to explore his sexuality. Eager to oblige, the *Naked Attraction* production team provided the elderly gentleman with a choice of male and female would-be dates. To my companion and my (and I think his own) surprise, our hero eventually plumped for one of the naked women on offer, a well-endowed lady of riper years. He chose her, he confided, both because he liked the look of her but also, and mainly, because during the show's unexpected craft section she had modelled her piece of soft clay into the shape of a huge heart instead of a gigantic phal—*

---

* We let that one run for an incredible uninterrupted 90 seconds because we were all so gripped.

ALMOST WINNING EURO 2020

Almost winning Euro 2020 is a not a reference to the Italian national football team's victory in that competition in '21, a year later than its billing, but to the heart-breaking disappointment of the runners-up: their opponents representing England, who hadn't won a major international contest for 55 years. So the chants that the round ball sport was 'coming home' may have sounded a trifle hollow at the beginning of the group stages, but they began to gather conviction and (dare one say?) hope as the side progressed towards the knock-out rounds. Aspirations for the seemingly impossible lurched towards delirious expectations when the home lads playing at Wembley in the Round of 16 beat arch rivals Germany 2–0. They trounced Ukraine by twice that margin in the quarters, overcame Denmark by a goal in the semis and entered the final itself with the country on tenterhooks. With the score tied at 1 all after extra time, the match went to penalties and the old nemesis struck, unlike spot kicks that failed to find the net – and the wait for a trophy continues.

SHOPPING ONLINE

Shopping online is what Christmas should be like: living the consumer dream all year round without the seasonal angst and no faux festive cheer. There you are, cocooned in your comfort zone, totally sheltered from the madding crowd, able to peruse at leisure whatever catches your fancy and snap it up with a simple click of the fingers – free of guilt at how much you've just spent because you know that when the bargain you couldn't resist is delivered 24 hours later, all you have to do is return it and the money zips back into your account. Shopping online also saves us the grim experience of real-life purchasing – battling around supermarkets with an overburdened trolley, grabbing stuff haphazardly from the shelves and then queuing for the checkout anxiously watching the clock because we penny-pinched on the parking charges. In a way, having the stuff brought to your front door is like Xmas too, but with less livestock and no synthetic goodwill. That's reserved for winning the National Lottery and the potential offered there takes shopping online to an unimaginable level – well, almost.

Oooh...
It's like
Christmas!

MY FANTASY PODCAST

Podcasts are a phenomenon of our time. Until 20 years ago, they weren't even a fantasy. No one had thought of them. They didn't exist. The name comes from an amalgamation of 'iPod' and 'broadcast', and from nowhere yesterday they're everywhere today. I do one all about words and language with my friend, the lexicographer, Susie Dent. We call it *Something Rhymes with Purple* because there is a word that does – 'hirple'. It means 'to walk with a limp'. In the near future I am planning to launch a new podcast series and this will be called *My Fantasy Podcast* because in it I will be talking to leading world figures about their secret fantasies. So far those who have agreed to be interviewed by me include Donald Trump, Vladimir Putin, Boris Johnson, the Pope, Ed Sheeran, Lewis Hamilton, Jeff Bezos, Kylie Jenner, Cristiano Ronaldo, Emma Raducanu and Dwayne Johnson, nicknamed 'The Rock', and reckoned, as of now, as the most famous person on the planet. Well, I told you it was called *My Fantasy Podcast*. I'm actually interviewing a guy who was briefly Kim Kardashian's PR agent and my friend Tim Vine, who is Jeremy's brother. I couldn't get Jezza, but Timothy is very funny. He's the fellow who said, 'Velcro – it's a rip-off.'

THE KETO DIET

The Keto diet started out in the twentieth century as a way of treating epilepsy in children; but it drew inspiration from ancient Greek doctors who adjusted the diet of patients with certain conditions, notably the one mentioned above. A hundred years ago physicians tried to control the same malady by getting sufferers to eat a low-carb diet; the idea being that this would force the body to derive energy from burning fats. The science behind it is quite complex and the jury is still out whether or not the Keto diet is as effective as its proponents would have everyone believe, but it crops up now and then when those in the know decide it's time for a new weight-loss craze. The Atkins diet (remember that?) was a kind of Keto (that's to say a ketogenic) diet, and it did its creator no harm: his diet-book became one of the top 50 best-selling ever. So, if you want to slim, give this diet a try. It could be your Keto success!

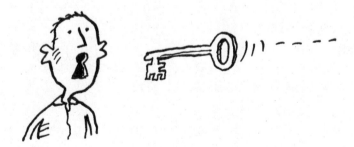

FORTNITE

Fortnite would be a little less baffling for the uninitiated if its creators had picked a different name. Given that its three modes are called *Fortnite: Save the World, Fortnite Battle Royale* and *Fortnite Creative,* one could be forgiven for assuming that *Fortknight* was some kind of Arthurian romance, written in Middle English, wrongly shelved for centuries gathering dust on a forgotten library shelf and only recently discovered. On the subject of the etymology of our native tongue, 'fortnight' of course refers to a two-week period of 14 nights, or *feowertiene niht* as it was termed when the older version of the language was in mode.* These days, of course, the very mention of *Fortnite* immediately registers with those in the know as the multi-award-winning video game created by Epic Games, which is enjoying a revenue stream pushing $10 billion – and *Fortnite* has only been available to gamers since the summer of 2017. It makes you speculate whether sales figures could be twice that if the sequel to *Fortnite* was called *Month.*

---

* It's clear that the author hasn't a clue what the subject in the title refers to. But he manages to busk it by prattling away about homophones while desperately trying to remember what the designated topic really is. The result is that over half the time elapses before he gets to the actual subject, by which time readers are bamboozled and the clock is ticking down to the end of the minute.

BEING POSITIVE ABOUT THE PANDEMIC

Being positive about the pandemic? Is such a thing possible? Probably only if, like me, you're a logophile – a lover of words. The COVID-19 pandemic took lives, brought about suffering, cost billions, certainly, but the upside is that it richly enriched our vocabularies. The word itself, pandemic, comes from the Greek – *pan* meaning 'all' and *demos* being 'local people' or a 'crowd'. A pandemic is an epidemic that has spread across a large region, affecting a substantial number of individuals. The coronavirus pandemic – also known as 'the 'rona' and the 'Miley' (as in Cyrus – cockney rhyming slang) – has led to a massive increase in the use of existing terms such as 'self-isolating', 'quarantine', 'lock-down' and 'key workers' and a glorious explosion in neologisms. My favourites include 'covidiot' (someone who ignores public health advice), 'covideo party' (an online get-together via Zoom or Skype) and 'covexit' (the strategy for exiting from the whole traumatic episode). 'Quarantinis' were cocktails served during the vid's darkest moments. 'Blursday' referenced the pandemic's disorientating effect on time. 'Zoombombing' described hijacking a videocall. 'WFH' was an initialism for 'working from home' and 'WTF' a perfectly legitimate reaction to the realisation that we're probably going to have to live with variations of this thingy forever.

Goodbye.

Last Word

by Sue Perkins

When I think of *Just A Minute*, I think of being a kid, maybe seven or eight, hearing it on the radio for the first time – the elastic vowels of Kenneth Williams, the laconic, nasal drawl of Clement Freud. To this day, I marvel at how such a simple game can embrace such breadth and complexity – the world in a grain of sand indeed. I have aged with the show; it's kept me company as I've got greyer and fatter and slower. It's a constant in the whirlwind of life. The panellists may have changed (though only a little) but the show has stayed as fresh as ever; kept buoyant by the decades-long steerage of the late, great Nicholas Parsons in the role of chair.

I was in my twenties when I first got to play the game myself. No word of a lie, being asked to be a part of this extraordinary show was like getting a nod from the Queen. The pressure was immense, and I seem to remember getting buzzed only a few seconds into my opening round. But on my second show I managed to run for the full minute – a sensation akin to flying. You can feel the audience bringing you up and willing you on. After that, the powers that be made it somewhat harder for me, and I remember distinctly gulping as I was given subjects such as String Theory and Dadaism ...

I mention the audience because they are such an integral part of the show. They take it as seriously, sometimes more so, than we do. They are invested in the newcomers, the old-timers, the running gags, the highs and lows, the hard calls and the benefits of the doubt. Most of all, like me, they want nothing more than the whistle to sound after someone has achieved that all-elusive minute.

Just A Minute sat on the shoulders of twin giants; Ian Messiter, creator of the game, and Nicholas, the man who made that game sing. Sadly, we have lost both. But Malcolm Messiter, Ian's son, still comes to the recordings to keep us on the straight and narrow, and Nicholas, well Nicholas is always in my ear.

The role of host was not one I accepted lightly. The shoes are impossible to fill. Nicholas is part of the very DNA of the show; it's near impossible to say the words 'as the Minute Waltz fades away ...' without tracing his exact cadence, recalling his rhythm and emphasis. I miss him.

I hope there are kids out there just starting to listen to our programme, perhaps even playing the game themselves at home or with friends. I hope one day I get to see a few of them on the show itself, cheering them uproariously when they complete their inaugural minute. In a world full of change and uncertainty I wouldn't be surprised if this radio parlour game isn't there at the very end, along with the cockroaches.

Welcome to
Just A Minute...

ACKNOWLEDGEMENTS

I should acknowledge my history teachers, both at school and at university, and I would, but my publishers think it a bit risky, in case they are still alive and want to sue me. Instead, let me acknowledge my friend, Clive Dickinson, writer and historian, for his guidance and support. He has taught me all the history I have learnt since we first met in Oxford forty years ago. I am also grateful to my friend Henry Dawe for sharing some of his favourite historic jokes with me and, of course, to my lovely *Just A Minute* friends, Sue Perkins, Shaparak Khorsandi and Josie Lawrence, for their contributions.

This book wouldn't have come into being at all if Ian Messiter hadn't devised *Just A Minute* all those years ago. I salute his memory with great affection and respect, and thank his family for allowing me to create this book. My heartfelt thanks, too, to the amazing BBC team behind *Just A Minute,* led by Julia McKenzie, formerly Creative Director at BBC Studios, and now Commissioning Editor of Comedy and Entertainment at Radio 4.

When I hosted my first panel game for Radio 4 in 1971, the producers were David Hatch and Simon Brett – the original producers of *Just A Minute.* When I first appeared on the show in the 1980s, the producers were Pete Atkin and Edward Taylor. Since then I have been lucky enough to appear in hundreds of episodes of the game (on radio and TV) and, over the years, the producers I have had fun working with – and learning from – include Chris Neill, Claire Jones, Tilusha Ghelani, Katie Tyrrell, Victoria Lloyd, Matt Stronge, Richard Morris, Alex Smith and Hayley Sterling. I am indebted to them all – and to their assistants: the indefatigable whistle-blowers. (Some, like Hayley Sterling, joined the *JAM* family as whistle-blowers and ended up in charge.)

All of us involved in *Just A Minute* do feel part of a family for a special reason: the head of the family, our father (who art now in heaven), the late, great Nicholas Parsons, who chaired the show for more than half a century, and was a friend, mentor and inspiration to us all. He's gone, but he's not forgotten, and he would be so happy that the show he loved so much continues with the brilliant Sue Perkins now happily at the helm. That's the joy of *Just A Minute*: it evolves and old stagers like me and my extraordinary friend, Dame Sheila Hancock, 90 this year and funnier than ever, are joined by brilliant newcomers, most of whom weren't even born when we first played the game.

This book is the brainchild of the great Albert DePetrillo (Publishing Director at BBC Books and Ebury) and I am indebted to him and to Nell Warner (my wonderful editor), Howard Watson (copy editor), Steve Tribe (proofreader) and Lisa Footit (indexer).

I think the book looks so good so I want to acknowledge Jonathan Baker (of Seagull Designs) for the text design, Jamie Keenan (of Keenan Designs) for the cover design and my genius friend Steven Appleby for the ace illustrations.

Once my friend and agent Jonathan Lloyd had done the deal (for which I send him 15 per cent of my thanks), Antony Heller in Production at BBC Books made it all happen, and if you have been lucky enough to have been given it (or have even bought it for yourself) that will be down to the efforts of Alice King and Lizzy Dorney (Publicity), Mia Oakley (Marketing), and the nonpareil sales team at BBC Books: Aslan Byrne, Hannah Grogan, Antony de Rienzo, Ben Green, Beth Stuart, Alison Pearce, Carl Rolfe, and Tracy Orchard. My thanks to them all.

Most of all, of course, my thanks go to you for having the book in your hand and for reading this now. I hope bits of it have made you smile. 'Life is a mirror,' wrote William Makepeace Thackeray, the author of *Vanity Fair*, 'if you frown at it, it frowns back; if you smile, it returns the greeting.'

Have a nice day!

Gyles Brandreth,
London, 2022

INDEX